Collins

AQA GCSE (9–1)
English Literature
and Language

A
Christmas
Carol

Student Guide

Mike Gould

William Collins' dream of knowledge for all began with the publication of his first book in 1819. A self-educated mill worker, he not only enriched millions of lives, but also founded a flourishing publishing house. Today, staying true to this spirit, Collins books are packed with inspiration, innovation and practical expertise. They place you at the centre of a world of possibility and give you exactly what you need to explore it.

Collins. Freedom to teach.

Published by Collins
An imprint of HarperCollinsPublishers
The News Building
1 London Bridge Street
London
SE1 9GF

Browse the complete Collins catalogue at
www.collins.co.uk

British Library Cataloguing in Publication Data

A catalogue record for this publication is available from the British Library.

Commissioned by Catherine Martin
Project managed by Hannah Dove and Natasha Paul
Developed by Caroline Low and Lesley Gray
Edited by Catherine Dakin
Proofread by Nikky Twyman
Photo research by Alison Prior
Cover design by Ink Tank
Cover images Classic Image/Alamy
Typesetting by Jouve India Private Limited
Illustrations by Beehive Illustration
Production by Rachel Weaver
Printed and bound in Italy by Grafica Veneta S.p.A.

Contents

Introduction

How to use this book

This Student Book is designed to support your classroom study of *A Christmas Carol*.

It offers an integrated approach to studying English Literature and English Language, to help you prepare for your AQA GCSE exams.

The book can be used as a 10-week programme, if desired, or dipped into throughout your course or for revision.

English Literature

The book includes a pre-reading chapter to introduce some of the novel's key contexts and concerns.

Six chapters then guide you through the novel in depth, with activities to build your understanding of the plot, themes, characters, language and structure of the novel.

At the end of your reading, two whole-text revision chapters revisit key themes, characters and contexts to help you form your own interpretations of the whole novel.

Each chapter opener page clearly shows you what you will read and explore for English Literature and for English Language.

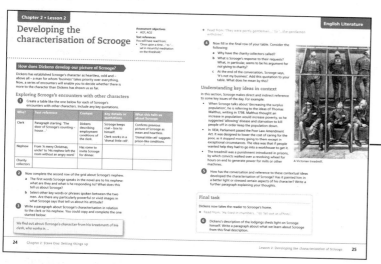

Literature lessons help you to engage with key scenes from the novel, building your analysis skills.

Finally, Chapter 10 focuses on your Paper 1 English Literature exam. Two practice questions are provided, with guidance to help you plan and write effectively. Sample responses with commentaries show you the difference between a clear and well-explained and a convincing, analytical answer.

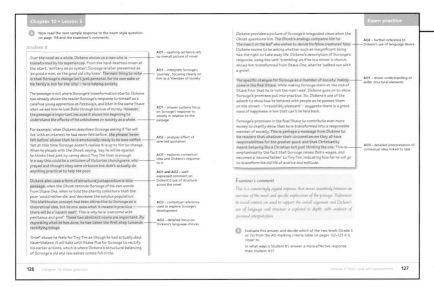

Practice questions and sample responses help you to prepare for assessment.

The closing page of each chapter offers a longer task on the text so far, to build your writing stamina for the final exam.

English Language

Each chapter also includes one or more lessons focused on building your English Language skills.

You will read fiction and non-fiction texts from the 19th, 20th and 21st centuries. These have been chosen to enhance your understanding of the themes and contexts of *A Christmas Carol*.

You will be given the opportunity to explore these texts and respond to them by answering questions in the style of the AQA Paper 1 and Paper 2 exams. Across the book, you will practise each of the AQA question types, including narrative, descriptive and discursive writing.

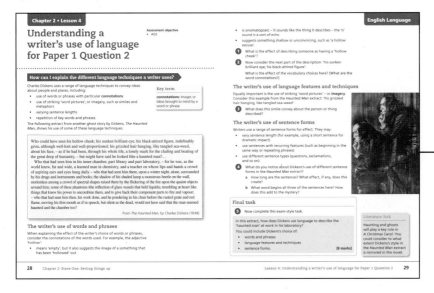

Language lessons will focus on one AQA question type. The text extracts have been chosen to deepen your understanding of the events, themes and contexts in this chapter of the novel. Literature link boxes make the connection to the novel clear.

Who's who? A guide to the main characters

Ebenezer Scrooge

- Scrooge is the main character in the story. Scrooge is a business man who is very miserly and values money above friendship, family or compassion for other people.

- Scrooge is the main focus of every Stave. We meet his younger selves in Stave Two and see his reformed character in Stave Five.

Fred

- Fred is Scrooge's nephew, the son of Scrooge's dead sister. Fred is a friendly, jovial character who treats others kindly. He tries to persuade Scrooge of the value of Christmas.

- Fred appears in Stave One and Stave Three, and his kindness towards Bob is mentioned in Stave Four.

Bob Cratchit

- Bob is Scrooge's clerk. He is poor and badly treated by Scrooge. He has a large family to support on a small wage, including his disabled child, Tiny Tim. He and his wife, Mrs Cratchit, are presented as loving parents.

- Bob appears in Stave One, Stave Three, Stave Four and Stave Five.

Marley's Ghost

- Jacob Marley was Scrooge's former business partner, who died several years before the story begins. Like Scrooge, he was obsessed with money.

- Marley appears as a ghost in Stave One to warn Scrooge not to make the same mistakes he did.

The Ghost of Christmas Past

- The first of the night-time visitors. This ghost has the face of a young child but the hair and body of an older man. He takes Scrooge to the key scenes of Scrooge's boyhood and early career to show him how he has changed.

- This Ghost appears in Stave Two.

Fanny

- Fanny is Scrooge's sister. She dies young, leaving behind one child, Scrooge's nephew Fred.

- Fanny appears in Stave Two, coming to fetch Scrooge home from school.

Mr Fezziwig

- Mr Fezziwig is Scrooge's first boss. He is a jolly, caring man who makes sure all his employees are happy.

- He appears in Stave Two.

Belle

- Belle is Scrooge's former fiancée. She breaks off her engagement with Scrooge when he becomes too obsessed with money. We see her go on to have a happy family life with another man.

- Both her appearances are in Stave Two.

The Ghost of Christmas Present

- The second spirit to visit Scrooge. He embodies the generosity and compassion of Christmas. He also criticises Scrooge for his attitude towards those less fortunate than himself.

- This Ghost appears in Stave Three.

Tiny Tim

- Tiny Tim is the son of Bob Cratchit. Tim has a crutch and his body is supported by an iron frame. He is presented as selfless and caring, despite his suffering.

- He appears in Stave Three and his death and its effects are foretold in Stave Four. In Stave Five we learn he does not die, thanks to Scrooge's change of heart.

Ignorance and Want

- These children represent the suffering of children without education, food or shelter in Victorian Britain. They also represent the likely consequences for society of their neglect.

- Ignorance and Want appear at the end of Stave Three.

The Ghost of Christmas Yet to Come

- This final spirit represents Death. He shows Scrooge what a lonely death he will have if he doesn't change his ways.

- He appears at the end of Stave Three but is the focus of action in Stave Four.

Stave summaries

Summary of Stave One

We meet Scrooge in his office on Christmas Eve. He is treating his clerk Bob Cratchit meanly.

Scrooge's nephew Fred calls in to wish his uncle a happy Christmas and to invite him to Christmas dinner. He is sent away with a lecture.

Two charity collectors arrive, asking for Christmas donations for the poor. Scrooge refuses to donate any money. He says there are already prisons and workhouses to support the poor.

Scrooge goes home to his lonely lodgings. At his front door, he sees the ghostly face of his dead business partner Jacob Marley where his door knocker should be. Refusing to believe what he sees, Scrooge goes in and makes himself supper.

The ghost of Marley then appears, loaded down with chains. He begs Scrooge to change his life while he still has the chance. As Marley leaves, he tells Scrooge that he will be haunted by three further spirits when the clock strikes twelve. Scrooge goes to bed.

Summary of Stave Two

At one o'clock in the morning, a strange figure appears at Scrooge's bedside. This is the Spirit of Christmas Past.

The spirit takes Scrooge back to his boyhood. At the fireside of the empty school Scrooge sits, all alone, reading a book.

In the next scene, the boy is older. His sister Fanny arrives to bring him home for Christmas. The older Scrooge thinks sadly of his sister's death. The ghost reminds him she left behind a child, his nephew Fred.

Now they move to Scrooge's first workplace: the kind Mr Fezziwig's office. Scrooge thinks guiltily of his clerk Bob Cratchit.

Finally, the Ghost shows him a scene with his former fiancée. Now a business man, she calls off their engagement, saying he is more interested in money. They see the same woman again some years later, married and surrounded by her children. Scrooge feels pain and regret. This could have been his life.

He begs the spirit to take him away.

Summary of Stave Three

The clock strikes one again. A voice calls him. Scrooge enters the next room and sees it brightly lit and filled with food and Christmas decorations. A giant man in green sits on top of the food. He is the Ghost of Christmas Present.

Scrooge and the Ghost head out over London. The Ghost shows him all kinds of happy Christmas scenes.

Then they are at the house of Bob Cratchit and his family. The children are very excited about the small dinner that is being prepared. Bob and his youngest son come in. Tiny Tim is disabled. Scrooge asks if he will live but the Ghost says he will not, unless something changes.

Scrooge and the Ghost pass through other scenes where Christmas is being celebrated: a mining town, a lonely lighthouse.

Then they are at Scrooge's nephew's house. It is a jolly scene. Scrooge is caught up in the games and asks to stay a little longer.

Scrooge and the Ghost travel further. Finally, Scrooge notices something beneath the Ghost's robes. A claw? A foot? Two tiny, ugly children are revealed. The Spirit tells Scrooge their names are Ignorance and Want, and they are Man's children.

As the clock strikes twelve again, the Ghost is gone. Another hooded figure approaches...

Summary of Stave Four

The hooded figure comes toward Scrooge. Scrooge asks, is this the Ghost of Christmas Yet to Come? The figure points him onwards.

They go to the centre of the City of London. A group of businessmen are talking about another man's death. There is some laughter but little sadness. Then they are in Scrooge's office but another man sits at his desk. Scrooge is puzzled.

Now they are in a poor, gloomy, dirty part of London. At a pawn shop, a cleaner, an undertaker and a washer woman have brought things to sell. They have been taken from a dead man's bed. Scrooge is horrified.

In the second half of Stave Four, things get even worse for Scrooge.

The Ghost takes him to the dead man's room. A body lies beneath a sheet. No friends or loved ones are there to mourn the death. The Spirit points to the body, gesturing for Scrooge to lift the sheet. Scrooge cannot. He still does not understand what the Ghost is showing him.

Scrooge asks to see someone who cares about the man's death. The Ghost takes him to a couple's house. They are happy the man has died, as they owed him money.

Finally, they go to the Cratchits' home. Tiny Tim has died and the family are grieving. Scrooge sees the effect of his death on the family who loved him so dearly. Bob says he has met Fred, Scrooge's nephew, and Fred had promised to help them.

Scrooge asks to see his own future. The Ghost shows him his office; another man is in his chair. The Ghost then takes him to a graveyard and points to a gravestone. The name on the stone is 'Ebenezer Scrooge'. Scrooge recoils from this vision of his own death. He promises to lead a better life.

Summary of Stave Five

Scrooge wakes up in his own bed. It is Christmas morning and he is still alive. He leaps out of bed and asks a boy in the street to buy the biggest turkey from the butcher's and take it to Bob Cratchit's house.

Out in the London streets, Scrooge wishes everyone he meets a happy Christmas. He sees the charity collector again and apologises for his rudeness the day before. He pledges a huge sum of money to the charity.

He then surprises Fred by joining him and his wife for Christmas lunch.

When Bob Cratchit comes to work the next day, Scrooge gives him a pay rise and promises to help his family.

The new Scrooge leads a happy and generous life. He remembers all the lessons the Ghosts have taught him and he is a second father to Tiny Tim, who does not die.

Chapter 1

Pre-reading: Dickens's life and times

English Literature

You will read:

- about Dickens's early life
- about the lives of children in Victorian England.

You will explore:

- what inspired Dickens to write *A Christmas Carol*.

English Language

You will read:

- a 19th-century, non-fiction extract by Henry Mayhew
- an extract from the novel *Oliver Twist* by Charles Dickens.

You will explore:

- what life was like for children on the streets or in the workhouse
- how to find key information in texts
- how to write your points concisely.

Charles Dickens – his formative years

Assessment objective
- AO3

··

How does knowledge about Dickens help my study of *A Christmas Carol*?

You will be expected to 'show understanding of the relationships between texts and *the **contexts** in which they were written*' (Assessment objective 3). This means, among other things, being able to demonstrate that you understand some of the ideas and events that influenced Charles Dickens's work.

Charles Dickens: his early life

1   Read this timeline of Dickens's life up until when he wrote *A Christmas Carol*.

> **Key terms**
> ···
> **context:** the social, cultural and historical influences on a writer or background to a text
>
> **blacking factory:** industrial building where pots of shoe polish are produced
>
> **pseudonym:** alternative name taken by a writer

Timeline

Born in Portsmouth to John and Elizabeth Dickens.

Dickens's father and family are sent to Marshalsea Prison for debtors. Charles is forced to leave school and work in a **blacking factory**.

Dickens begins work at a solicitors' office, but soon starts writing as a freelance reporter.

In April, Dickens marries Catherine Hogarth. In the same month, his first full novel, *The Pickwick Papers*, is published.

A Christmas Carol is published.

| 1812 | 1815 | 1824 | 1825 | 1827 | 1833 | 1836 | 1837–41 | 1843 |

Family moves to London, then to Chatham in Kent, before returning to London.

Dickens goes back to school, but the headmaster is brutal and the teaching poor.

Dickens becomes a parliamentary journalist for the *Morning Chronicle*. His contacts in the press help him publish a series of sketches under the **pseudonym** 'Boz'.

Four new novels published, including *Oliver Twist and Nicholas Nickleby*, both in serial form.

2   What kind of childhood did Dickens have? How would you say Dickens's early life differed from his life after 1827?

Influential experiences

3   Dickens writes about his childhood experiences both directly, in recalling his childhood, and through some of his novels.

Read the three extracts on page 13. Select one and make notes on:

- what we learn about Dickens's experiences
- how he communicates these ideas. (What words and phrases does he use?)

School life

There were little faces which should have been handsome, darkened with the scowl of sullen, dogged suffering; there was childhood with the light of its eye quenched, its beauty gone, and its helplessness alone remaining; there were vicious-faced boys, brooding, with leaden eyes, like malefactors in a jail.

From *Nicholas Nickleby*,
by Charles Dickens (1839)

The blacking factory

It was a crazy, tumble-down old house, abutting of course on the river, and literally overrun with rats. Its wainscoted rooms, and its rotten floors and staircase, and the old grey rats swarming down in the cellars, and the sound of their squeaking and scuffling coming up the stairs at all times, and the dirt and decay of the place, rise up visibly before me, as if I were there again.

Dickens's recollections, quoted in *The Life of Charles Dickens*, by James Forster

Dickens, exhausted, at his desk in the blacking factory.

Trying to make ends meet

I know that I worked, from morning to night, with common men and boys, a shabby child. I know that I tried, but ineffectually, not to anticipate my money, and to make it last the week through; by putting it away in a drawer I had in the counting-house, wrapped into six little parcels, each parcel containing the same amount and labelled with a different day. I know that I have lounged about the streets, insufficiently and unsatisfactorily fed. I know that, but for the mercy of God, I might easily have been, for any care that was taken of me, a little robber or a little vagabond.

Dickens's recollections, quoted in *The Life of Charles Dickens*, by James Forster

Final task

The mistreatment and misfortune children face are key themes in Dickens's work, including *A Christmas Carol*.

 Write 60–75 words explaining the impression Dickens gives of life for poor children in these extracts.

Why Dickens wrote
A Christmas Carol

Assessment objective
- AO3

How was Dickens influenced by social issues of the time?

While Dickens's own childhood influenced his writing, it was what he heard about and experienced as an adult that prompted him to write *A Christmas Carol*.

 Read the following extracts and, as you do so, think about what convinced Dickens to put pen to paper.

Children's Employment Commission

In 1842, the Children's Employment Commission produced their second Parliamentary Report into the conditions children and women were working under throughout the country. Here is one extract, about metal manufacture in Sedgley, near Birmingham:

> Children are first put to labour from the ages of seven to eight, where they continue at work daily from six o'clock in the morning till seven or eight at night, and on weigh-days, the days the nails are taken to the factors, from three or four in the morning till nine at night… Their food at the same time is in general insufficient, their clothing miserable, and the wretchedness of their dwellings almost unparalleled.

The Industrial Revolution

Much of the misery recorded in the report was the result of the revolution in manufacturing in the Victorian period (1819–1901). Previously, most goods had been produced in people's homes in small numbers. New machinery that could be operated in factories meant high volumes of goods could be produced (mass production). This led to a flow of workers from rural communities to cities. The iron, steel and textile industries were at the heart of this industrial revolution, with cities such as Manchester becoming centres of production with enormous cotton mills and large workforces.

The workhouse or the streets

Wages were very low, and the work could be dangerous. Young children were often used for hazardous jobs such as cleaning machinery; there were few safety measures and little if any protection against redundancy. The need for large workforces led to cities growing rapidly and with them slums – desperately poor, dirty and crowded areas where the most disadvantaged people lived.

2 Look at the image above of workers in a cotton mill.

- What do you notice about their age and clothing?
- What dangers do you think they would have faced?

The alternatives to working in such factories for poorer children were to beg, to earn money from selling cheap items (flowers, buttons, and so on), to be driven into prostitution or to enter a workhouse. Workhouses were large buildings intended as a sort of refuge for the poorest, but these disease-ridden and over-crowded places were more like prisons. It was hoped their awful conditions would deter able-bodied people from entering them and claiming 'poor relief'.

3 Why might Dickens have been particularly sensitive to the sort of life children faced in factories?

Dickens's response

Having read the Employment Commissioners' report and been 'perfectly stricken down by it', in October 1843 Dickens gave a fundraising speech at the first annual general meeting of the Manchester Athenaeum (an adult education institute for the working class). It was while he was in this industrial town, staying with his older sister, Fan, one of whose two young sons was frail and disabled, that he came up with the idea for the novel *A Christmas Carol*. Dickens wrote of the book being like a 'sledgehammer' that 'will come down' on those responsible for the poor laws. Dickens wanted to 'strike the heaviest blow' in his power to raise awareness of the conditions of the poor, and especially working children.

Final task

Dickens had originally intended to publish a 'pamphlet' (a sort of persuasive leaflet) in response to the Employment Commissioners' report, but decided instead on a story.

4 Make notes on why you think Dickens:

- chose the story format rather than a leaflet or speech
- decided a Christmas story was particularly appropriate for what he wanted to say about the suffering of children.

Identifying information for Paper 2 Question 1

Assessment objective
• AO1

What skills do I need to draw out key information from a text?

Dickens was not the only person concerned about the plight of the poor. Henry Mayhew (1812–87) was a social reformer, journalist and playwright who researched the lives of many of London's working class and unemployed.

Account of a Victorian child street seller

In order to find out specific information about a child's life, read the following account, which Mayhew heard from a 9-year-old girl.

Glossary

from the parish: money or food given by the local church

ha'porth: a shortening of 'half penny worth'

It's in the winter, sir, when things are far worst with us. Father can make very little then but I don't know what he earns exactly at any time – and though mother has more work then, there's fire and candle to pay for. We were very badly off last winter, and worse, I think, the winter before. Father sometimes came home and had made nothing, and if mother had no work in hand
5   we went to bed to save fire and candle, if it was ever so soon. Father would die afore he would let mother take as much as a loaf **from the parish**. I was sent out to sell nuts first: 'If it's only 1d you make,' mother said, 'it's a good piece of bread.' I didn't mind being sent out. I knew children that sold things in the streets. Perhaps I liked it better than staying at home without a fire and with nothing to do, and if I went out I saw other children busy. No, I wasn't a bit frightened when I first
10   started, not a bit. Some children – but they was such little things – said: 'O, Liz, I wish I was you.' I had twelve **ha'porths** and sold them all. I don't know what it made; 2d most likely. I didn't crack a single nut myself. I was fond of them then, but I don't care for them now. I could do better if I went into public-houses, but I'm only let go to Mr Smith's, because he knows father, and Mrs Smith and him recommends me and wouldn't let anybody mislest me. Nobody ever offered
15   to. I hear people swear there sometimes, but it's not at me. I sell nuts to children in the streets, and laces to young women. I have sold nuts and oranges to soldiers.

    I don't know what I shall be when I grow up. I can read a little. I've been to church five or six times in my life. I should go oftener and so would mother, if we had clothes.

From *London's Labour and London's Poor*, by Henry Mayhew (1851)

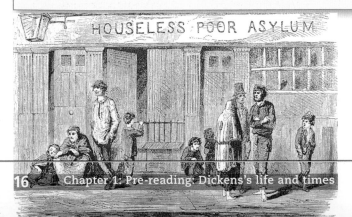

HOUSELESS POOR ASYLUM

Scanning for key information

Question 1 of your English Language Paper 2 exam will ask you to read a text and then decide whether statements about that text are 'true'. To do this, you need to be able to **scan** the text for key words, in order to check the statement's accuracy.

For example, for the Henry Mayhew text, if you were given the statement: 'The girl's father occasionally earned nothing during the day', you would need to:

- scan the text for the word 'father'
- read the whole sentence and information around the reference to 'father', to establish clearly what is being said
- decide whether the information you have found supports the statement
- continue scanning and checking the text, until you have checked all references to 'father' and can make a final decision about the accuracy of the statement.

1 Use the guidance above to work out whether the statement 'The girl's father occasionally earned nothing during the day' is true.

2 Which of the following statements about the girl's father are also true?

  a The father makes more money in the winter.

  b The father objects to the girl's mother taking things 'from the parish'.

  c The father would go more regularly to church if he had suitable clothing.

Final task

3 Now complete this exam-style task.

Read again the source from line 3 to the end.

Choose **four** statements below which are TRUE.

Choose a maximum of four statements.

a In a bad winter, the girl goes to bed early to save using up candles.

b The first thing the girl sold was nuts.

c The girl was a bit frightened when she first started street selling.

d The only pub the girl can go to is Mr Smith's.

e The girl sells oranges and laces to soldiers.

f The girl has been to church only five or six times in her life so far. **[4 marks]**

Literature link

In *A Christmas Carol*, you will read an account of a poor family who, like this one, try to remain respectable despite their poverty. These are versions of the poor as represented by Mayhew and Dickens. Look out for other descriptions that are not as sympathetic to the poor.

Identifying and recording information for Paper 1 Question 1

Assessment objective
- AO1

How do I write or note down key points in the most efficient way?

Dickens's most famous account of life for Victorian children in the workhouse comes in his novel, *Oliver Twist,* published between 1838 and 1839.

An extract from *Oliver Twist*

As you read the extract below, think about the portrayal of the boys and how hungry they are.

> **Glossary**
>
> **copper:** big pot
> **porringer:** bowl

The room in which the boys were fed was a large stone hall, with a **copper** at one end, out of which the master, dressed in an apron for the purpose, and assisted by one or two women, ladled the gruel at meal-times. Of which composition each boy had one **porringer**, and no more – except on festive occasions, and then he had two ounces and a quarter of bread besides. The bowls never wanted washing – the boys polished them with their spoons till they shone again; and when they had performed this operation (which never took very long, the spoons being nearly as large as the bowls), they would sit staring at the copper, with such eager eyes, as if they could have devoured the very bricks of which it was composed; employing themselves, meanwhile, in sucking their fingers most assiduously, with the view of catching up any stray splashes of gruel that might have been cast thereon. Boys have generally excellent appetites. Oliver Twist and his companions suffered the tortures of slow starvation for three months: at last they got so voracious and wild with hunger, that one boy, who was tall for his age, and hadn't been used to that sort of thing (for his father had kept a small cookshop), hinted darkly to his companions, that unless he had another basin of gruel *per diem*, he was afraid he might some night happen to eat the boy who slept next him, who happened to be a weakly youth of tender age. He had a wild, hungry eye; and they implicitly believed him. A council was held; lots were cast who should walk up to the master after supper that evening, and ask for more; and it fell to Oliver Twist.

The evening arrived: the boys took their places; the master in his cook's uniform stationed himself at the copper; his pauper assistants ranged themselves behind him; the gruel was served out; and a long grace was said over the short commons. The gruel disappeared, and the boys whispered each other and winked at Oliver, while his next neighbours nudged him. Child as he was, he was desperate with hunger and reckless with misery. He rose from the table, and advancing, basin and spoon in hand, to the master, said, somewhat alarmed at his own temerity—

'Please, sir, I want some more.'

From *Oliver Twist*, by Charles Dickens (1838)

1 In the extract, what overall impression is given of the food and how the boys view it?

Use the scanning skills you developed in Lesson 1.3 (pages 16–17) to look for particular references to the food, how the boys eat it and their feelings about it.

Identifying and noting down key information

Question 1 of English Language Paper 1 not only asks you to *find* the correct information but also to *note it down*. You can:

- present your information in short, concise sentences or in bullet form
- quote directly from the text or briefly paraphrase (put it in your own words).

For example, if you were asked to list what you were told about the boys in the first few lines of the extract (down to 'cast thereon'), you could write:

Oliver asking for more; this illustration by George Cruikshank appeared in the original edition of *Oliver Twist*.

> *each had one porringer, and no more*
>
> or:
>
> *The boys were given only one bowl of food.*

2 Jot down a further point about how the boys ate their food.

Final task

3 Now complete this exam-style task.

Read again the extract from 'Oliver Twist and his companions…' to the end.

List four things from this part of the text about Oliver. **[4 marks]**

Checklist for success

✔ Scan for references to Oliver.

✔ Stick to information about him.

✔ Use bullet points or short sentences either to quote directly (if clear) or to paraphrase (make the points in your own words).

Literature link

From this extract and the earlier extracts from Dickens's work, you should be gaining a sense of Dickens's writing style. One aspect of this is to mix humorous description with grim realities. How is this done in the extract?

End of chapter task

London

It is often said that London is itself a character in Dickens's novels. But what was London like then?

First, it is worth bearing in mind London's huge growth: in 1800 it had about one million inhabitants, but by 1900 the population had grown to about 6.7 million, making London, for a time, the largest city in the world. However, many of its population lived in poverty. Despite – and indeed because of – the advances made by industry, London could be an unhealthy and dangerous place. It suffered from terrible fogs, worsened by the fumes and smoke from factories and chimneys, and it wasn't until the end of the 19th century that a proper sewer system was developed.

A contemporary of Dickens, Arthur Morrison, described a part of East London called 'the Jago' in this way:

> The narrow street was all the blacker for the lurid sky; for there was a fire in a further part of Shoreditch, and the **welkin** was an infernal coppery glare. Below, the hot heavy air lay, a rank oppression, on the contorted forms of those who made for sleep on the pavement: and in it, and through it all, there rose from the foul earth and grimed walls a close, mingled stink, the odour of the Jago.
>
> From *A Child of the Jago*, by Arthur Morrison (1897)

 Divide a page into two down the middle and on the left side write 'Impressions of London from other works', and on the right 'Impressions of London from *A Christmas Carol*'. Complete the left-hand column based on the information and the texts you have read in this chapter. Then, as you read the novel *A Christmas Carol,* complete the right-hand column, seeing whether these impressions of London are carried through in the novel or whether an alternative version of the city emerges.

Check your progress

- I can show clear understanding of the contextual factors that influenced Dickens's work.

- I can show thoughtful consideration of the contextual factors that influenced Dickens's work.

Glossary

welkin: sky or heaven

Chapter 2

Stave One: Setting things up

English Literature

You will read:

- Stave One of *A Christmas Carol.*

You will explore:

- how writers create characters
- your first impressions of Scrooge
- how the theme of ghosts and the supernatural is introduced
- the function of the supernatural in the novel.

English Language

You will read:

- an extract from the short story *The Haunted Man* by Charles Dickens.

You will explore:

- how writers use language to create effects
- how to write about language techniques and effects.

How Dickens introduces Scrooge

Assessment objectives
- AO2, AO3

Text references
You will have read from:
- the start of the novel to 'was what the knowing ones call "nuts" to Scrooge.'

How does Dickens engage our interest in the story and the main character?

A Christmas Carol is subtitled 'A ghost story of Christmas'. This helps to set the **tone** and create expectations, as does the introduction of the main character.

How does the title of A Christmas Carol work?

It helps to think about the tone and **form** of what we are about to read. For example:

- 'Christmas' locates the tale at a particular time of year – and Christmas is intended as a time of love, goodwill and of new birth.
- 'Carol' is a particular type of song for Christmas, historically created for the common people to share in a celebratory, everyday fashion.

1 Make notes on what you expect from the story. Consider:
- what the use of the word 'ghost' in the subtitle suggests about the story to follow
- why you think Dickens chose the word 'stave' rather than 'chapter'? (Look up the meaning of this word if you do not know it.)

2 Now read the opening paragraph of *A Christmas Carol* and make further notes on:
- **a** how the opening sentence (especially the clause *after* the colon) engages our interest
- **b** how the certainty of Marley's death is made clear in the remaining sentences (think about the final **simile** of the paragraph)
- **c** how the opening seems slightly at odds with the title of the story. In what way could it appear **ironic** (at this point)?

First impressions: Scrooge

3 How does Dickens portray Scrooge at the start of the novel? Use these questions to help you.
- What are we told directly about a character (by the narrator/ writer and the particular language choices)?
- What can we **infer** from the character's appearance, behaviour and speech?

Key terms

tone: the particular mood or feeling conveyed

form: a type or genre of text

simile: a comparison between two things using 'like' or 'as'

ironic: seeming to create the opposite effect of what might have been intended

infer: work out from clues rather than from what is explained directly

- What can we infer from the settings or locations (such as home or place of work) associated with the character?
- What can we learn from their interactions (behaviour, speech, and so on) with other characters?

Understanding direct information and making wider inferences

Even seemingly unimportant details can be revealing. For example, the very first mention of Scrooge is 'Scrooge signed it' (meaning the register of the burial of Marley, Scrooge's business partner). This is important because:

- Scrooge's first act is a grim, legal one
- he is happy to put his name to the fact of Marley's death.

4 Can you infer anything else about Scrooge from these facts? Is he a lawyer? A doctor? Perhaps we need more information.

Work through the text that follows and gather evidence. Think about:

- What *other* facts are we told about Scrooge in the paragraph starting 'Scrooge knew he was dead?'
- What is the significance of Scrooge making a profitable business deal on 'the very day of the funeral?'

5 Why do you think Scrooge 'never painted out Old Marley's name'? Write a sentence explaining your ideas, referring to any clues from the text.

Final task

◆ Read from 'Oh! But he was a tight-fisted hand at the grindstone, Scrooge!' to '...is better than an evil eye, dark master!'

6 Make detailed notes about the language used to describe in this passage. You could comment on:

- the image of Scrooge given in the very first sentence, and the connotations from it
- the adjectives ending '–ing': are these positive or negative?
- the effect of the two similes: 'hard and sharp as flint' and 'solitary as an oyster'
- the cause of his 'shrivelled' cheek, 'stiffened' way of walking and his 'grating' voice. (Be careful – it is not the cold weather!)
- the **extended metaphor** continued in the final sentence of the paragraph.

Key term

extended metaphor: a comparison developed in several ways along the same lines

Developing the characterisation of Scrooge

Assessment objectives
- AO1, AO2

Text references
You will have read from:
- 'Once upon a time…' to '…sat in mournful meditation on the threshold.'

How does Dickens develop our picture of Scrooge?

Dickens has established Scrooge's character as heartless, cold and – above all – a man for whom 'business' takes priority over everything. Now, a series of encounters will enable you to decide whether there is more to the character than Dickens has shown us so far.

Exploring Scrooge's encounters with other characters

1 Create a table like the one below for each of Scrooge's encounters with other characters. Include any key quotations.

Who?	Text reference	Context	Key details or quotations	What this tells us about Scrooge
Clerk	Paragraph starting: 'The door of Scrooge's counting – house…'	Dickens describing employment conditions of the clerk.	Scrooge keeps coal – box to himself. Clerk works in a 'dismal little cell'.	Confirms previous picture of Scrooge as mean and heartless. 'Dismal little cell' suggests prison-like conditions.
Nephew	From 'A merry Christmas, uncle!' to 'His nephew left the room without an angry word.'	Has come to invite Scrooge for dinner.		
Charity collectors				

2 Now complete the second row of the grid about Scrooge's nephew.

  a The first words Scrooge speaks in the novel are to his nephew: what are they and what is he responding to? What does this tell us about Scrooge?

  b Select other key words or phrases spoken between the two men. Are there any particularly powerful or vivid images in what Scrooge says that tell us about his attitude?

3 Write a paragraph about Scrooge's characterisation in relation to the clerk or his nephew. You could copy and complete the one started below:

> We find out about Scrooge's character from his treatment of his clerk, who works in…

◆ Read from: 'They were portly gentlemen...' to '...the gentlemen withdrew'.

4 Now fill in the final row of your table. Consider the following:

a Why have the charity collectors called?

b What is Scrooge's response to their requests? What, in particular, seems to be his argument for *not* giving to charity?

c At the end of the conversation, Scrooge says, 'It's not my business'. Add this quotation to your table. What does he mean by this?

Understanding key ideas in context

In this section, Scrooge makes direct and indirect reference to some key issues of the day. For example:

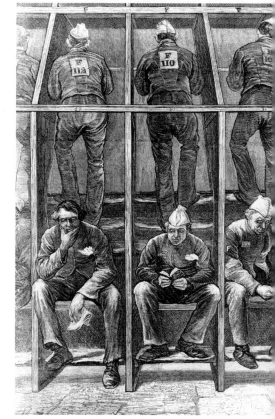

A Victorian treadmill.

- When Scrooge talks about 'decreasing the surplus population', he is referring to the ideas of Thomas Malthus, writing in 1798. Malthus thought an increase in population would increase poverty, so he suggested 'allowing' disease and starvation to kill people off in order keep the population down.

- In 1834, Parliament passed the Poor Law Amendment Act. It was designed to lower the cost of caring for the poor, as it stopped money going to them except in exceptional circumstances. The idea was that if people wanted help they had to go into a workhouse to get it.

- The treadmill was a punishment introduced in prisons, by which convicts walked over a revolving wheel for hours on end to generate power for mills or other machines.

5 How has the conversation and reference to these contextual ideas developed the characterisation of Scrooge? Has it painted him in a better light or stressed certain aspects of his character? Write a further paragraph explaining your thoughts.

Final task

Dickens now takes the reader to Scrooge's home.

◆ Read from: 'He lived in chambers...' to 'let out as offices'.

6 Dickens's description of the lodgings sheds light on Scrooge himself. Write a paragraph about what we learn about Scrooge from this final description.

Marley's Ghost: introducing the supernatural

Assessment objectives
- AO1, AO2

Text references
You will have read from:
- Marley's appearance as a 'door-knocker' to the end of Stave One.

How does Dickens use linguistic and structural devices to convey the supernatural?

The first part of Stave One introduced Scrooge and his mean nature, yet a different type of story was foreshadowed by the very first sentence.

Structuring the supernatural

> Key term
>
> **minor sentence:** a word or phrase that acts as a sentence but which is not grammatically complete (for example, it omits the subject)

◆ Read from 'Scrooge, having his key in the lock of the door...' to "Humbug!" said Scrooge; and walked across the room.'

In this section of the text, Dickens uses a variety of language and structural devices to introduce the supernatural.

1 Read the four paragraphs listed in the left column of the table, then complete the final two rows of the table.

Paragraph	Use of language and structure	Effect
'Marley's face...' to '...part of its own expression'	Short, **minor sentence** sets up paragraph – the face is the focus. References to the light Marley's face emits. Repetition of 'ghostly' and 'horror'/'horrible', and the simile 'like a bad lobster in a dark cellar'.	Sense-related descriptions fix the image in our mind. Simile suggests something rotten and decaying but, importantly, *hidden away*. Marley's appearance is unnatural and disturbing: hair 'curiously stirred', eyes 'motionless'.
'As Scrooge...again'	Short, one–sentence paragraph. Focus is back on Scrooge; the vision disappears. Choice of scientific-sounding word 'phenomenon'.	The suddenness of it switching back to 'normal' matches the abrupt nature of the paragraph. Suggests the supernatural could be a figment of Scrooge's imagination.
'To say...' to 'lighted his candle'	Deals with how Scrooge responds to the vision. But he turns the key 'sturdily'.	Conveys Scrooge's...
'He *did* pause...' to 'closed it with a bang'		

Detective work

As the novel progresses, there will be many occasions where we, like Scrooge, have to work out what something *means*. Think of it as assembling clues about Scrooge's state of mind or Dickens's themes.

2 Consider the different pieces of evidence below and discuss each 'exhibit' in turn in pairs or groups.

Exhibit A: the vision of the hearse

- Whose body might be on it?
- Or is it on the way to collect a body? If so, whose?

Keep any notes you make for later reference.

Exhibit B: Marley's Ghost and his chains

◆ Read from 'His colour changed...' to "You will be haunted," resumed the Ghost, "by Three Spirits".'

This is a very important section of the book. Pay attention in particular to Marley's appearance and what he says, and keep in mind his function.

- What items are on the chain? What do they seem to **symbolise**? (Check their qualities – physical properties, look, weight.)
- Do they link to anything mentioned earlier in the Stave?
- What effect do they have on Marley?

The Ghost's words are important evidence in understanding the function of the supernatural in *A Christmas Carol*. In response to Scrooge's statement that Marley was a good man of 'business', the Ghost replies:

> 'Mankind was my business. The common welfare was my business; charity, mercy, forbearance, and benevolence, were, all, my business. The dealings of my trade were but a drop of water in the comprehensive ocean of my business!'

3 Based on this, and any other evidence from the Stave, what do you think the purpose of Marley's Ghost's visit is? How does it link back to Scrooge's words and actions earlier in the Stave?

Final task

4 Go over Stave One as a whole and trace Scrooge's responses to the supernatural from the moment he sees the knocker until the Ghost departs. How does Scrooge change? Select specific words or phrases that show his initial response as well as his later ones.

Understanding a writer's use of language for Paper 1 Question 2

Assessment objective
- AO2

How can I explain the different language techniques a writer uses?

Charles Dickens uses a range of language techniques to convey ideas about people and places, including:

- use of words or phrases with particular **connotations**
- use of striking 'word pictures', or imagery, such as similes and metaphors
- varying sentence lengths
- repetition of key words and phrases.

The following extract from another ghost story by Dickens, *The Haunted Man*, shows his use of some of these language techniques.

> **Key term**
>
> **connotations:** images or ideas brought to mind by a word or phrase

Who could have seen his hollow cheek; his sunken brilliant eye; his black-attired figure, indefinably grim, although well-knit and well-proportioned; his grizzled hair hanging, like tangled sea-weed, about his face, – as if he had been, through his whole life, a lonely mark for the chafing and beating of the great deep of humanity, – but might have said he looked like a haunted man?…

Who that had seen him in his inner chamber, part library and part laboratory, – for he was, as the world knew, far and wide, a learned man in chemistry, and a teacher on whose lips and hands a crowd of aspiring ears and eyes hung daily – who that had seen him there, upon a winter night, alone, surrounded by his drugs and instruments and books; the shadow of his shaded lamp a monstrous beetle on the wall, motionless among a crowd of spectral shapes raised there by the flickering of the fire upon the quaint objects around him; some of these phantoms (the reflection of glass vessels that held liquids), trembling at heart like things that knew his power to uncombine them, and to give back their component parts to fire and vapour; – who that had seen him then, his work done, and he pondering in his chair before the rusted grate and red flame, moving his thin mouth as if in speech, but silent as the dead, would not have said that the man seemed haunted and the chamber too?

From *The Haunted Man*, by Charles Dickens (1848)

The writer's use of words and phrases

When explaining the effect of the writer's choice of words or phrases, consider the connotations of the words used. For example, the adjective 'hollow':

- means 'empty', but it also suggests the image of a something that has been 'hollowed' out

- is onomatopoeic – it sounds like the thing it describes – the 'o' sound is a sort of echo
- suggests something shallow or unconvincing, such as 'a hollow excuse'.

1 What is the effect of describing someone as having a 'hollow cheek'?

2 Now consider the next part of the description: 'his sunken brilliant eye; his black-attired figure'.

What is the effect of the vocabulary choices here? (What are the word connotations?)

The writer's use of language features and techniques

Equally important is the use of striking 'word pictures' – or **imagery**. Consider this example from the *Haunted Man* extract: 'his grizzled hair hanging, like tangled sea-weed'.

3 What does this simile convey about the person or thing described?

The writer's use of sentence forms

Writers use a range of sentence forms for effect. They may:

- vary sentence length (for example, using a short sentence for dramatic impact)
- use sentences with recurring features (such as beginning in the same way or repeating phrases)
- use different sentence types (questions, exclamations, and so on).

4 What do you notice about Dickens's use of different sentence forms in the *Haunted Man* extract?

a How long are the sentences? What effect, if any, does this create?

b What word begins all three of the sentences here? How does this add to the mystery?

Final task

5 Now complete this exam-style task.

In this extract, how does Dickens use language to describe the 'haunted man' at work in his laboratory?

You could include Dickens's choice of:

- words and phrases
- language features and techniques
- sentence forms.   **[8 marks]**

Literature link

Haunting and ghosts will play a key role in *A Christmas Carol*. You could consider to what extent Dickens's style in the *Haunted Man* extract is mirrored in the novel.

End of chapter task

Look at this extract taken from Stave One, when a boy approaches Scrooge's office. Complete the task that follows.

The owner of one scant young nose, gnawed and mumbled by the hungry cold as bones are gnawed by dogs, stooped down at Scrooge's keyhole to regale him with a Christmas carol: but at the first sound of

'God bless you, merry gentleman!
May nothing you dismay!'

Scrooge seized the ruler with such energy of action, that the singer fled in terror, leaving the keyhole to the fog and even more congenial frost.

At length the hour of shutting up the counting-house arrived. With an ill-will Scrooge dismounted from his stool, and tacitly admitted the fact to the expectant clerk in the Tank, who instantly snuffed his candle out, and put on his hat.

'You'll want all day to-morrow, I suppose?' said Scrooge.

'If quite convenient, sir.'

'It's not convenient,' said Scrooge, 'and it's not fair. If I was to stop half-a-crown for it, you'd think yourself ill–used, I'll be bound?'

The clerk smiled faintly.

'And yet,' said Scrooge, 'you don't think *me* ill–used when I pay a day's wages for no work.'

The clerk observed that it was only once a year.

'A poor excuse for picking a man's pocket every twenty-fifth of December!' said Scrooge, buttoning his great-coat to the chin. 'But I suppose you must have the whole day. Be here all the earlier next morning.'

The clerk promised that he would; and Scrooge walked out with a growl.

---

1 How does Dickens present Scrooge as a mean and unpleasant character in this extract?

Write about:

- in what ways Scrooge could be considered 'mean' and 'unpleasant'
- the methods Dickens uses to present Scrooge.

Check your progress

- I can select appropriate references when explaining my ideas.
- I can explain Dickens's methods clearly and some of their effects on the reader.

- I can select precise references when analysing the text.
- I can explore in detail the methods Dickens uses and how these engage or interest the reader.

Chapter 3

Stave Two: Developing themes and ideas

English Literature

You will read:

- Stave Two of *A Christmas Carol*.

You will explore:

- Dickens's use of language, narrative perspective and voice to advance key themes
- how Dickens explores the influence of the past (childhood and education) on the present.

English Language

You will read:

- a letter written by Dickens, in which he explores the education of the poor
- a 20th-century non-fiction extract, in which an author recalls her experiences of school in the late 1940s.

You will explore:

- how to identify, interpret and summarise information from two related texts
- how to identify key information related to a task
- how to express relevant points in a concise and efficient way.

The function of the Ghost of Christmas Past

Assessment objectives
- AO2, AO3

Text references
You will have read from:
- the start of Stave Two to 'And he sobbed.'

What is the function of the Ghost of Christmas Past in the story?

A different sort of Spirit

While Marley's Ghost seemed fairly traditional – with clanking chains, dire warnings – the Ghost of Christmas Past, who now appears to Scrooge, is somewhat different.

◆ Read from the opening of Stave Two to "I am a mortal," Scrooge remonstrated, "and liable to fall."

Dickens manages to **embody** what the Spirit represents in a number of ways. Consider some of the key descriptions of it:

> - 'It was a strange figure – like a child: yet not so like a child as like an old man…'
> - 'It held a branch of fresh green holly in its hand; and, in singular contradiction of that wintry emblem, had its dress trimmed with summer flowers.'
> - '…what was light one instant, at another time was dark, so the figure fluctuated in its distinctness…'

1 What is notable about the **juxtaposition** of ideas in each of these pairs of descriptions? Consider:

   a How similar or different is each image in each description?

   b How does each set of pairs in one sense or another represent memory, and/or time passing or passed?

2 Why might Dickens have chosen to represent the Ghost in a way that links it to pagan figures?

3 In this part of the text, the Ghost explains his role directly to Scrooge as part of a 'question and answer' session.

   a What does this Spirit tell Scrooge he represents? How is this linked to the Spirit's appearance?

   b What does the Spirit say his purpose is? How is this matched by the Spirit's general tone and behaviour?

Key terms

embody: give expression or physical form to an idea or feeling

juxtaposition: the careful placing together of ideas or images to create an effect

---

Key context

In the references to holly and summer flowers, the Ghost might be linked to pagan (pre-Christian) figures such as the Green Man, who symbolises rebirth after the darkness of winter and the coming of spring.

How we respond to the Spirit and Scrooge's conversations

As the Stave progresses, Dickens establishes a key **motif** that runs through the text: the writer as informed, **ironic observer**. Events or descriptions that we (as readers) understand clearly come slowly to Scrooge.

However, as we see Scrooge respond to the Spirit, our attitude towards Scrooge may begin to change. This is due to a number of elements, such as Dickens's use of humour.

4 When the Ghost mentions his purpose is Scrooge's 'welfare', what could Scrooge 'not help thinking'?

5 What is slightly comical about Scrooge's situation when the Spirit commands him to 'Rise! and walk with me!'?

In both cases, Dickens reveals Scrooge's inner thoughts – his **interiority** – while continuing to give us a broader picture of events. This enables us to see the world increasingly as Scrooge experiences and reacts to it, rather than as we did at the start of the novel, when we observed Scrooge in a more distant way.

> **Key terms**
>
> **motif:** a recurring idea in an artistic work
>
> **ironic observer:** a narrator who comments in an amused, sometimes critical way on the actions of characters
>
> **interiority:** inner life

The use of questioning

◆ Read from 'Bear but a touch of my hand there' to 'And he sobbed.'

In this section, the Ghost continually questions Scrooge – as if trying to get him to respond in a particular way.

6 Think again about the Green Man and the idea of rebirth.

  a What words or phrases suggest that the Spirit's 'gentle touch' has reawakened feelings buried deep in Scrooge's cold heart?

  b What questions does the Spirit ask, and how does Scrooge respond?

  c Look in particular at the paragraph starting 'The jocund travellers came on…' How do the descriptions of Scrooge's appearance and actions show a change from his earlier depiction in the novel?

Final task

 7 Write about the ways that Dickens uses the Ghost of Christmas Past at the start of the Stave to begin to alter our understanding of Scrooge. Consider:

- how the Ghost shows its kindly side to Scrooge

- how Scrooge's responses to the Ghost make us more sympathetic to him.

Exploring the theme of how childhood experiences influence later life

Assessment objectives
• AO1, AO2

Text references
You will have read from:
• 'The school is not quite deserted...' to 'My time grows short.'

Why does the Spirit show Scrooge his past life as a schoolboy and apprentice?

In Lesson 4 of this chapter, you will find out more about the 'Ragged Schools' that existed in Dickens's day. These were often harsh places that provided for the education of poorer children. Dickens himself was sent away to school – not to a Ragged School, but to a private school. In Stave Two of *A Christmas Carol*, Dickens draws on these experiences to evoke Scrooge's past.

A picture of school life

◆ Read from 'The school is not quite deserted...' to '...and gave a freer passage to his tears'.

1. What sort of place is the school? Using the information in the table, locate each place in the text and then jot down the particular words and phrases Dickens uses to describe it.

The construction of the 'mansion'	The 'spacious offices'	The 'coach-houses and sheds'	The 'many rooms' near the hall
Dull, red brick			

2. Here, a student has written about one particular phrase describing the school setting:

apt quotation

analysis of language use

In this section, Dickens describes the 'leafless boughs of one despondent poplar'. Through personifying the sad tree through the adjective 'despondent' and through its barren appearance, Dickens links the cold, depressing setting to Scrooge's situation as a child. In this way, Dickens develops the theme of education or childhood influencing later life, as readers recall the older Scrooge's cold and uninviting manner in Stave One.

links analysis to exploration of the theme

link to earlier part of novel

Choose a word, phrase or short sentence of your own and explain its effects in a similar way.

3. Why does Scrooge sob (and later weep) when he sees himself as he was back then?

4 When the young Scrooge and Fan discuss their father, what impression are we given of Scrooge's childhood? Refer closely to the text in your answer.

5 How do both these examples alter our attitude to Scrooge?

Dickens's use of a mirroring structure to develop themes

In Stave Two, we begin to see Dickens introduce echoes of earlier events in the novel. Through this, we see how the Ghost re-educates Scrooge by asking him to reflect on details and incidents from Stave One.

6 Copy and complete this table.

Stave One: Scrooge's treatment of children	Stave Two: Scrooge's sympathy for children
Scrooge chases away a carol singer who 'fled in…'	Scrooge refers to this incident when he…

◆ Read from 'Always a delicate creature…' to 'wished him or her a Merry Christmas'.

7 How does the Ghost use the example of Fezziwig to re-educate Scrooge about the need for companionship and kindness?

- Look at the depiction of the party at Scrooge's old employer, Fezziwig.

- Then create a table like the one below to record ideas about Scrooge's workplace in Stave One and Fezziwig's workplace in Stave Two. You could add examples of how each employer treats their employees and others.

Stave One: Scrooge's workplace at Christmas	Stave Two: Fezziwig's workplace at Christmas
Mood: cold, uninviting, static and few people	Mood:
Quotations:	Quotations:

Final task

◆ Read from: "A small matter," said the Ghost' to 'My time grows short.'

8 In this section, Scrooge responds in an animated way to the Ghost's gently provocative comments. He says:

- (about Fezziwig) 'He has the power to render us happy or unhappy…The happiness he gives, is quite as great as if it cost a fortune.'

- (about his clerk) 'I should like to be able to say a word or two to my clerk just now.'

a How do these two statements link back to Scrooge's attitude and behaviour in Stave One?

b What do they suggest about Scrooge's new understanding of what is truly valuable?

Developing the theme of what is really valuable in life

Assessment objectives
• AO1, AO2
Text references
You will have read from:
• 'My time grows short...' to '...and forced him to observe what happened next.'

> **What does Scrooge learn about his past life and the consequences of his decisions?**

As we saw in the first part of Stave Two, Dickens used the device of the younger versions of Scrooge, and the current, older Scrooge who observes, to explore ideas about childhood and how past cruelty and kindness impact on the future. In this final part of the Stave, Dickens uses the same device again.

Symbols and metaphors

This time, Scrooge witnesses the defining moment of his relationship with his fiancée, Belle. So how does Dickens convey the particular characteristics of this younger Scrooge?

1 Read the following extract, then make notes on the questions that follow.

> He was older now; a man in the prime of life. His face had not the harsh and rigid lines of later years; but it had begun to wear the signs of care and avarice. There was an eager, greedy, restless motion in the eye, which showed the passion that had taken root, and where the shadow of the growing tree would fall.

a What do the two abstract terms 'care' and **'avarice'** mean here? ('Care' here may have a slightly different meaning from how the word is used today.)

b What metaphor is used in the second sentence? What sort of 'growth' (in Scrooge) is being referred to here, and how will it cast a shadow in the future?

Key terms

avarice: valuing money over other things

2 After this, Belle says that a 'golden' idol has taken her place in Scrooge's affections.

• What does she mean?

• What does Scrooge give as his reason for worshipping such an idol?

3 What is Scrooge's new 'passion', according to Belle?

4 What are the consequences of this change in Scrooge that Belle has observed?

Ideas about 'value' as explored through Belle

We learn little of Belle as a real person or character in this section. However, we do find out that she and Scrooge were poor when they first met and fell in love.

5 We are also told that Belle is 'in a mourning-dress' and is 'a **dowerless** girl'. What do these two details suggest about Belle's personal status and financial circumstances?

6 What sort of impact might this have on their relationship, given what Belle has said about Scrooge? What is he choosing to 'value' here?

◆ Read from 'They were in another scene and place…' to the end of the Stave.

This section of the text takes Scrooge to a place where he observes Belle, in later life, married and with her husband. Here, Belle is characterised in more depth.

7 How does Dickens link this section with what has gone before? Think about how Scrooge might now measure the 'value' of what he is shown. Complete this paragraph:

> The exciting, joyful family scene is contrasted in several ways with earlier ones. For a start, we cannot help visualising Belle's meeting with Scrooge when…
>
> The contrast drawn by Belle's husband of seeing Scrooge in his office also highlights different ideas about what is valuable in life. Scrooge is busy earning money, but is described as…

Glossary

dowerless: in the Victorian period it was expected that middle-class women would be given a dowry (here 'dower' – money or property) from their parents, which would become their husband's on marriage

Final task

After the arrival of Belle's husband, Dickens writes:

> And now Scrooge looked on more attentively than ever, when the master of the house, having his daughter leaning fondly on him, sat down with her and her mother at his own fireside; and when he thought that such another creature, quite as graceful and as full of promise, might have called him father, and been a spring-time in the haggard winter of his life, his sight grew very dim indeed.

8 How does Dickens explore the idea of the consequences of avarice in this extract?

Write a paragraph explaining:

- how Scrooge reacts to what he sees
- the imagery used to explain its effect on him (think about the idea of rebirth, and what children can represent).

Summarising ideas from texts for Paper 2 Question 2

Assessment objective
• AO1

How can I summarise ideas from texts?

In this Lesson, you will read:

• a letter written by Dickens, in which he explores the education of the poor (something that is central to this Stave)

• another more modern text, which discusses aspects of school life.

What key skills will I need?

The key skills you will need are the ability to:

• select key information and present it in a statement

• support your ideas with evidence in the form of a quotation

• show your understanding through inference.

The extract on page 39 is from a letter Charles Dickens wrote to a newspaper in 1846. In his letter, Dickens complains about the state of a school for the poor (a so-called **Ragged School**) that he visited.

1 Read the extract. As you read, consider what you find out about the pupils – you will use this information in a later task. Remember:

• focus on selecting the key information about the pupils, not anyone else.

Key context

Ragged Schools

Non-paying schools set up by charitable institutions in the late 18th and early 19th centuries for the poorest children (those 'raggedly clothed'). While the intentions of their supporters might have been sound, the conditions in the schools were often appalling.

Glossary

the Deity: God

It consisted at that time of either two or three – I forget which – miserable rooms, upstairs in a miserable house. In the best of these, the pupils in the female school were being taught to read and write; and though there were among the number, many wretched creatures steeped in degradation to the lips, they were tolerably quiet, and listened with apparent earnestness and patience to their instructors. The appearance of this room was sad and melancholy, of course – how could it be otherwise! – but, on the whole, encouraging.

The close, low chamber at the back, in which the boys were crowded, was so foul and stifling as to be, at first, almost insupportable. But its moral aspect was so far worse than its physical, that this was soon forgotten. Huddled together on a bench about the room, and shown out by some flaring candles stuck against the walls, were a crowd of boys, varying from mere infants to young men; sellers of fruit, herbs, lucifer-matches, flints; sleepers under the dry arches of bridges; young thieves and beggars – with nothing natural to youth about them: with nothing frank, ingenuous, or pleasant in their faces; low-browed, vicious, cunning, wicked; abandoned of all help but this; speeding downward to destruction; and UNUTTERABLY IGNORANT.

This, Reader, was one room as full as it could hold; but these were only grains in sample of a Multitude that are perpetually sifting through these schools; in sample of a Multitude who had within them once, and perhaps have now, the elements of men as good as you or I, and maybe infinitely better; in sample of a Multitude among whose doomed and sinful ranks (oh, think of this, and think of them!) the child of any man upon this earth, however lofty his degree, must, as by Destiny and Fate, be found, if, at its birth, it were consigned to such an infancy and nurture, as these fallen creatures had!
This was the Class I saw at the Ragged School. They could not be trusted with books; they could only be instructed orally; they were difficult of reduction to anything like attention, obedience, or decent behaviour; their benighted ignorance in reference to **the Deity**, or to any social duty (how could they guess at any social duty, being so discarded by all social teachers but the gaoler and the hangman!) was terrible to see.

From a letter by Charles Dickens that appeared in the *Daily News*, 4 February 1846

2 What are we told about the *pupils* in the first paragraph?
To decide:

- go through each line of the paragraph
- identify the *key information* Dickens tells us.

For example:

- First sentence: they were taught in 'miserable rooms'.
- Second sentence starts: 'In the best of these, the pupils in the female school were being taught to read and write.' So the girls get the better rooms.
- Your inference from the above might be: the girls are treated more favourably, perhaps due to their behaviour.
- Your summary point might be:

> We learn that the children were taught in 'miserable rooms' but the girls get the better of the 'miserable rooms' while being taught to read and write. This suggests the girls are treated more favourably than the boys, perhaps because of their behaviour.

3 Now write down two more things we find out about the female pupils from the opening paragraph. Write them as statements, with evidence – and try to make an inference in each case. For example, you could start:

> The girls work quietly and seem to pay attention to their teachers, as the writer states they were...

4 Read the rest of the extract and note down any other information you find out about the other pupils. You could use a table like the one below.

Evidence/quotation	Explanation (statement)	Inference

Different ideas about education

The extract below is taken from *Bad Blood* (2000) by Lorna Sage, in which she recalls her life growing up in the late 1940s and early 1950s. Like Dickens's letter, Sage's account describes pupils at a school, although in this case the author is one of them. In the extract, the author describes her infant school experiences.

Glossary

Hanmer: village in Wales

tribes: groups of related children at the school who stick together

5 Read the extract. As you read, focus on selecting the key information *about the pupils*, not anyone else.

We'd have seemed a lumpen lot: sullen, unresponsive, cowed, shy or giggly in the presence of grown-ups. A bunch of nose-pickers and nail-biters, with scabbed knees, warts, chapped skin and unbrushed teeth. We shared a certain family resemblance, in other words. Some of it was absolutely, organically, real: seven or eight huge families accounted between them for nearly half the population of the school. There were brothers, sisters and cousins who slapped, shoved and bossed each other unmercifully, but always stood up for their own flesh and blood… in the end.

…Having big brothers or (much better) big sisters – since the big boys had their own separate playground and didn't usually deign to intervene – seemed the first condition for survival in the infants' class. In fact, though, these rough, protective clans were already on the way out. There were quite a few parents who'd worked out that one way of escaping poverty was to have fewer children, and a subtle eye could have detected among the mass of rowdy, runny-nosed urchins a small sub-class of better-dressed, prissier and slightly more respectable children. The girls wore hair-slides and newly knitted cardigans, the boys were 'nesh' (the **Hanmer** word for anything from clean to feeling-the-cold to cowardly) and were endlessly tormented. Being an only child – as I was, for the time being – was a mixed blessing at best when it came down to the gritty realities of the playground. The 'nesh' ones I despised and it was entirely mutual, since I was dirty, precocious and had never been treated like a child. And the **tribes** despised me for being sole, pseudo-clean and 'stuck up'.

So the playground was hell: Chinese burns, pinches, slaps and kicks and horrible games. I can still hear the noise of a thick wet skipping rope slapping the ground. There'd be a big girl each end and you had to leap through without tripping. Joining in was only marginally less awful than being left out.

From *Bad Blood,* by Lorna Sage (2000)

At the end of this lesson, you will complete an exam-style task that requires you to use details from both extracts to summarise the differences between the pupils in the two schools.

You have already made some notes about the pupils from the 'Ragged School' that Dickens described in his letter. Now it is time to make some notes about the pupils in the *Bad Blood* extract.

6 Read through the *Bad Blood* extract and note down any direct information the writer tells us about the pupils. For example:

- 'A bunch of nose-pickers and nail-biters, with scabbed knees, warts, chapped skin and unbrushed teeth.'

Then think about how you can turn this information into concise comments about the pupils. For example:

- 'The children at Lorna Sage's school look unpleasant and their behaviour is unpleasant too.'

7 Now consider whether there are any points of difference between the children in Dickens's text and those in the *Bad Blood* extract. For example:

- Does Dickens comment about the pupils' appearance? Is he as direct and detailed about their bad habits as Sage is when describing the pupils in her school?

- How do the girls seem to behave in Lorna Sage's text? Is this comparable with the girls in Dickens's letter?

- What does Lorna Sage say about the boys? How does this contrast with Dickens's observations?

- Are the children all from the same background or social level in Sage's school? How does this compare with the children in the Ragged School that Dickens describes?

Final task

8 Now complete this exam-style task.

There are eight marks available for this question in the exam, so try to find at least four different things to say about each text.

> You need to refer to **both extracts** for this question. Use details from **both** extracts. Write a summary of the differences between the pupils in the two schools. **[8 marks]**

Checklist for success

✔ Only use quotes or refer to points about the pupils.

✔ Be concise – do not quote at length or make long, repetitive references to the texts.

✔ State what is explicit, but also look for what can be inferred.

End of chapter task

Read this extract from the end of Stave Two, in which Belle's husband mentions having seen Scrooge.

> 'I passed his office window; and as it was not shut up, and he had a candle inside, I could scarcely help seeing him. His partner lies upon the point of death, I hear; and there he sat alone. Quite alone in the world, I do believe.'
>
> 'Spirit!' said Scrooge in a broken voice, 'remove me from this place.'
>
> 'I told you these were shadows of the things that have been,' said the Ghost. 'That they are what they are, do not blame me!'
>
> 'Remove me!' Scrooge exclaimed. 'I cannot bear it!'
>
> He turned upon the Ghost, and seeing that it looked upon him with a face, in which in some strange way there were fragments of all the faces it had shown him, wrestled with it.
>
> 'Leave me! Take me back. Haunt me no longer!'
>
> In the struggle, if that can be called a struggle in which the Ghost with no visible resistance on its own part was undisturbed by any effort of its adversary, Scrooge observed that its light was burning high and bright; and dimly connecting that with its influence over him, he seized the extinguisher-cap, and by a sudden action pressed it down upon its head.
>
> The Spirit dropped beneath it, so that the extinguisher covered its whole form; but though Scrooge pressed it down with all his force, he could not hide the light: which streamed from under it, in an unbroken flood upon the ground.

1 How does Dickens present Scrooge's feelings of suffering and regret:
- in this extract
- in the novel so far?

Check your progress

- I can select appropriate references when explaining my ideas.
- I can explain some of the key themes of the novel clearly.

- I can select precise references when analysing the text.
- I can explore and analyse key themes in a convincing and detailed way.

Stave Three: Alternative lives

English Literature

You will read:

- Stave Three of *A Christmas Carol.*

You will explore:

- how Dickens uses structure to develop alternative versions of Christmas
- how Dickens develops the theme of poverty and deprivation
- how Dickens uses symbolism to convey his message.

English Language

You will read:

- an extract from the novel *The Woman in White* by Wilkie Collins.

You will explore:

- how a writer structures a text to interest the reader.

How writers structure texts for Paper 1 Question 3

Assessment objective
- AO2

What specific structural methods do writers use?

In Stave One of *A Christmas Carol*, a sentence at the end of a long paragraph sees Dickens 'zoom in' on the face of Marley on the knocker. Then we watch Scrooge from a distance as he moves around his lodgings. Longer descriptive sections (such as the one about the fireplace) and sentences follow, building elaborate detail and shifting our attention once again. This is structure – how and when the writer shifts our focus from one thing to another, to reveal information and engage our interest.

In your English Language Paper, you will be asked to comment on an unfamiliar text and the writer's use of structure. So, what should you look for?

Method A: focusing on a topic in particular paragraphs

Generally, writers use paragraphs to focus on one subject – even if the writer's treatment of that subject includes several different elements. For example, the long paragraph about Scrooge's fireplace in Stave One is all about the fire and the tiled fireplace that surrounds it.

Method B: zooming in, zooming out

When describing the fireplace in the example above, Dickens zooms in on the individual design on the tiles: 'Apostles putting off to sea in butter–boats'. Yet, at other points, Dickens zooms out and gives us a much wider vision. For example, at the end of the scene with Marley's Ghost, Dickens describes how 'The air was filled with phantoms, wandering hither and thither in restless haste'. Here, we are seeing the phantoms at a distance – their whole beings – rather being shown a specific phantom or any particular feature.

Method C: indicating time, place or perspective

Writers naturally wish to move the reader forward in time, flash back or indicate the order and sequence of events. This can be done:

- simply by moving to a new scene through a new paragraph
- by using connectives of time or place, such as 'later', 'many years earlier' or 'in another part of town'

- by using connectives such as 'yet' and 'however' to signal a shift in focus or a character's perception
- through use of tenses. For example, the past simple 'Scrooge *walked* across the room' gives a clear, immediate idea of an action, whereas the past perfect form 'Scrooge *had* often *heard* it said...' refers to more distant (in time) past thoughts and actions.

Method D: style and length of sentences and paragraphs

Watch for changes in the style and length of sentences and paragraphs – and their effects: perhaps to reflect, speed things up or accumulate detail and powerful imagery. For example:

- The short minor sentence in Stave One – 'Marley's face' – suggests Scrooge's shock, and the reader's too. The repetition of 'Marley's face' indicates the need to revisit what has been seen, as though asking, 'Can this be true?' The style, too – with no verb – is punchy and focused, like the impact of the face.
- Sentences that have multiple clauses, or that repeat conjunctions such as 'and', can build a bigger picture through a cumulative effect. For example, in Stave Two, notice the long sentence that evokes the joy of Fezziwig's party: 'There were more dances, and there were forfeits, and more dances, and there was cake, and there was negus, and there was a great piece of Cold Roast, and there was a great piece of Cold Boiled, and there were mince-pies, and plenty of beer.'

Method E: dialogue

Using speech can have a range of effects:
- Most notably, it tends to bring action and immediacy to stories.
- Speech often uses present tense forms ('"What do you *want* with me?" said Scrooge') and this alone can invite the reader into the moment.
- Dialogue can be structured in a range of ways – from 'ping-pong' – style question and response to more elaborate, reflective speeches and talk.
- Short lines of dialogue and lack of explanation can create mystery or tension; longer monologues or explanations can move the story forward or serve to articulate or explain events.

tting this into practice

Dickens's contemporary and friend, Wilkie Collins, was a master of the mystery story. Like Dickens, Collins sustains the reader's interest through his use of structure.

Read the following extract, which comes from early on in Collins's novel, *The Woman in White*.

I had now arrived at that particular point of my walk where four roads met – the road to Hampstead, along which I had returned, the road to Finchley, the road to West End, and the road back to London. I had mechanically turned in this latter direction, and was strolling along the lonely high-road – idly wondering, I remember, what the Cumberland young ladies would look like – when, in one moment, every drop of blood in my body was brought to a stop by the touch of a hand laid lightly and suddenly on my shoulder from behind me.

I turned on the instant, with my fingers tightening round the handle of my stick.

There, in the middle of the broad bright high-road – there, as if it had that moment sprung out of the earth or dropped from the heaven – stood the figure of a solitary Woman, dressed from head to foot in white garments, her face bent in grave inquiry on mine, her hand pointing to the dark cloud over London, as I faced her.

I was far too seriously startled by the suddenness with which this extraordinary apparition stood before me, in the dead of night and in that lonely place, to ask what she wanted. The strange woman spoke first.

'Is that the road to London?' she said.

I looked attentively at her, as she put that singular question to me. It was then nearly one o'clock. All I could discern distinctly by the moonlight was a colourless, youthful face, meagre and sharp to look at about the cheeks and chin; large, grave, wistfully attentive eyes; nervous, uncertain lips; and light hair of a pale, brownish-yellow hue. There was nothing wild, nothing immodest in her manner: it was quiet and self-controlled, a little melancholy and a little touched by suspicion; not exactly the manner of a lady, and, at the same time, not the manner of a woman in the humblest rank of life. The voice, little as I had yet heard of it, had something curiously still and mechanical in its tones, and the utterance was remarkably rapid.

From *The Woman in White* by Wilkie Collins (1859)

Literature link

Collins's zooming in on the woman's hand on the narrator's shoulder in *The Woman in White* is similar to the way Dickens focused our attention on Marley's face on the door-knocker in Stave One. Continue to look out for these 'framed moments' as you read the rest of *A Christmas Carol*.

Moving through the text

You are likely to be asked, in your English Language Paper, about what the writer focuses your attention on at the start of the text.

1 What is the focus in the first paragraph of the extract from *The Woman in White*?

   a Think about the overall situation. Where is the narrator? What can you picture in your mind?

   b What changes and shifts our attention as readers? What is the key phrase that makes us 'zoom in' on the narrator?

2 In the third paragraph, the attention shifts again away from the narrator's thoughts.

   a What does he *now* focus on – and why?

   b What is the *effect* of the main image in the second paragraph on both the reader and the narrator?

3 In the fourth paragraph, there is another change. The narrator now focuses on trying to explain, or sum up, how he feels. What words and phrases signal his state of mind at this point?

4 In the fifth paragraph of the extract, the woman asks a question.

   a What, and how much, does she say? What is the significance of her asking a question?

   b How does what she says add to or change the direction or mood of the text?

5 Can you identify how these structural features are used in the text?

   • time and place references are these sequenced in an order that is easy to follow, or do they disrupt the narration in some way?

   • connectives of time

   • connectives to mark a shift in the narrator's focus or perceptions

   What effect or function do these structural features have?

Final task

6 Now complete this exam-style task, which is based on the extract from *The Woman in White*.

> This text is from the opening of a novel.
> How has the writer structured the text to interest you as a reader?
> You could write about:
> • what the writer focuses your attention on at the beginning
> • how and why the writer changes this focus as the text develops
> • any other structural features that interest you.   **[8 marks]**

Structuring Christmas

Assessment objectives
- AO1, AO2

Text references
You will have read from:
- the start of Stave Three to '… Christmas daws to peck at if they chose.'

How does Dickens use structure to develop alternative visions of Christmas?

In Stave Two, the reader's attention was drawn to the contrast between Fezziwig's generous approach to his employees and Scrooge's mistreatment of Bob Cratchit in Stave One. In Stave Three, Dickens develops further contrasts and links – this time between alternative visions of Christmas.

Dickens's use of mirroring between Stave One and Stave Three

Stave Three opens with Scrooge discovering the Ghost of Christmas Present in the adjacent room.

◆ Read from: 'The walls and ceiling were so hung with living green…' to 'Come in! and know me better, man!'

1 We have already seen Scrooge's cold, mean and isolated version of Christmas in Stave One. In this section, how do Dickens's language choices help to build an alternative vision of Christmas?

    a What do the adjectives in phrases such as 'living green', 'bright gleaming berries' and 'crisp leaves' convey? What emotions or feelings do they suggest? How does this compare with Scrooge's idea of Christmas in Stave One?

    b How does the description of the fire in Stave Three contrast with its earlier description on Christmas Eve? (Look for the **noun phrases** such as 'mighty blaze'.)

    c There are at least three other references to light and its effect in the passage.

      • What is the general impression created by these descriptions of light?

      • What might light symbolise here? (For example, does it simply refer to the brightness of the room? Or, by contrasting with the darkness of Scrooge's home, does the light take on a different significance?)

> **Key term**
>
> **noun phrases:** phrases usually consisting of supporting words such as an adjective (or adjectives) added to a noun: for example, 'a strange [adj], inexplicable [adj] dread [n]'

Dickens's use of sentence structure

Consider the style of this sentence from Stave One, which describes Scrooge's sitting room on Christmas Eve.

> Nobody under the table, nobody under the sofa; a small fire in the grate; spoon and basin ready; and the little saucepan of gruel (Scrooge had a cold in the head) upon the hob.

The sentence is made up of compact phrases with simple nouns, to convey the sparse and basic food and implements.

2 Now consider the style of the long sentence in Stave Three beginning: 'Heaped up on the floor...'

What impression of Christmas is created by the sentence's language and structure, and how does this compare with the idea of Christmas created by the sentence from Stave One? You could write about:

- the listing of items and the effect this creates
- the appeal of the senses in the descriptions of particular foods ('juicy oranges')
- the use of personification in the 'cherry-cheeked apples'.

You could begin your answer:

> In Stave Three, the impression created by the 'throne' of food is very different to that of Scrooge's gruel and saucepan in Stave One. For example…

3 In this part of Stave Three, the Ghost of Christmas Present is described as having a 'capacious breast', 'genial face' and 'cheery voice'. The ghost also has an 'antique scabbard' *without* a sword.

What overall impression do these descriptions of the Ghost convey? For example, is there any significance in the Ghost's 'breast' being bared? (Try to find appropriate adjectives for expressing your ideas – for example, would 'friendly' be an appropriate description?)

◆ Read from 'Touch my robe!...' to '...daws to peck at if they chose.'

4 Make brief notes on how Dickens evokes other images of Christmas in this section.

Final task

5 How does Dickens use structural contrasts between Stave One and the opening of Stave Three to present alternative visions of Christmas?

- Include at least two examples of how Christmas is presented in each case.
- Add a comment in your conclusion about why Dickens has presented a vision of Christmas in Stave Three that contrasts with Scrooge's vision of Christmas in Stave One.

Shifting tones

Assessment objective
• AO2

Text references
You will have read from:
• 'In time the bells ceased...' to 'especially on Tiny Tim, until the last'.

How does Dickens use different methods to develop his thematic ideas?

In the first part of this Stave, Scrooge is shown alternative versions of Christmas. However, while they move him, they do not – as yet – resonate with him on a deeply personal level. This all changes when the Ghost of Christmas Present takes him to the Cratchits' home.

Creating empathy

For Dickens to convince his readers about the need to address poverty and deprivation, it was important for them to engage with the lives of the poor. Empathy is the ability on the part of the reader to understand why and how someone behaves in the way they do, and – in some circumstances – to feel their pain.

◆ Read from: 'Then up rose Mrs Cratchit...' to '...and trembling cast his eyes upon the ground.'

1 Consider these descriptions of the effects of poverty from this section.
  • 'dressed out but poorly in a twice-turned gown, but brave in ribbons, which are cheap' (Mrs Cratchit)
  • His 'threadbare clothes darned up and brushed, to look seasonable' (Bob)
  • 'Nobody said or thought it was at all a small pudding for a large family'
  • Peter's 'monstrous shirt collar (Bob's private property...)'
  a Discuss each description in turn. What impression does it give of the family, or the person described? Are readers meant to feel admiration, pity, shame – or some other response?
  b One student wrote about the first example:

> As readers, we understand Mrs Cratchit's desire to wear something special on Christmas Day, even if they are only ribbons, 'which are cheap'. However, it is sad that these cannot hide her poor clothing and her 'twice-turned gown'. Dickens wishes us to admire her resilience in the face of poverty.

Write a similar explanation of one of the other descriptions.

Tracing a change in tone

◆ Read from 'He sat very close to his father's side...' to '...cast his eyes upon the ground.'

Key term

tone: the attitude or feeling a writer creates (for example, comic, sad, ironic)

So far, the Cratchits' poverty has been presented in a gently humorous way, but now there is a change in **tone**.

2 Look at the examples in the table. Copy and complete the table, explaining the linguistic features and their effects on the mood.

Example from the text	Linguistic feature	Effect
'Bob held his withered little hand in his...dreaded that he might be taken from him.'	'Withered' is a vivid image of illness, normally associated with old age rather than childhood. 'Dreaded' tells us Bob's underlying state of mind.	Ominous – introduces a new, darker tone.
'I see a vacant seat... the child will die.'	Use of the modal verb 'will'...	
'If he be like to die... decrease the surplus population.'	Mirroring of...?	

An altered Scrooge?

At this moment, we see a turning point in Scrooge's behaviour. When Scrooge asks about Tim, it is with 'an interest he had never felt before'. Then, on hearing the Ghost's response, he is 'overcome with penitence and grief'.

3 Select particular words or phrases from this section and explain what they imply about Scrooge. For example, what does the powerful word 'overcome' tell us about Scrooge's feelings at this point?

4 What is different in the tone of the Ghost's final, longer speech here ('"Man," said the Ghost...' to 'brothers in the dust!')? How does this match with the change in the overall tone of the chapter?

Final task

◆ Read the final paragraph dealing with the Cratchits, from 'There was nothing of high mark in this....' to '...especially on Tiny Tim, until the last.'

5 Write at least two paragraphs explaining how Dickens has tried to influence the reader's response to ideas about poverty in this part of *A Christmas Carol*.

Checklist for success

✔ Comment on Dickens's presentation of the Cratchits and how we, as readers, respond to them.

✔ Consider how ideas about poverty (particularly those of Scrooge in Stave One) are questioned in Stave Three.

Understanding Dickens's use of symbolism

Assessment objectives
- AO2, AO3

Text references
You will have read from:
- 'By this time it was getting dark…' to the end of Stave Three.

What is symbolism, and how does Dickens use it to convey his message?

Further representations of Christmas

In this next section of Stave Three, Scrooge is taken to see a variety of scenes, from the dwellings of miners to a lighthouse, to a ship at sea and, finally, to his nephew Fred's. In each of these scenes, new ideas about Christmas are advanced or previous ideas are developed. In all these cases, you might say that the descriptions act in a **symbolic** way.

Some students have discussed why Dickens shows the two lighthouse men on the 'dismal reef of sunken rocks'. This is what they said:

> **Key term**
>
> **symbolic:** representing a wider idea or theme

> I think the depiction symbolises the power of Christmas to make people happy wherever they are.

> I think it's more than that – isn't it about humanity? How, whatever our condition or position in life, we can bless each other… I mean, there's the mention of his 'horny hands', like Jesus blessing the lepers…

> That's not really about Christmas, though, is it? The whole point is that this is one time, at least, when we can be nice to each other… don't forget this is about Scrooge.

1 What do you think? Do you agree with any of these students' ideas? What evidence can you find to support them?

Figures as symbols

You have already explored the way certain characters in the novel are largely symbolic. The Ghosts of Christmas Past and Present demonstrate this:

- their names are symbolic, representing time
- their appearances represent ideas: for example, the changing old/young face of the first Ghost shows that we are the products of our past lives, and the rich food and drink of the Ghost of Christmas Present's throne indicate the happy, generous sort of celebration Christmas can be.

◆ Read from "Forgive me if I am not..." to 'The bell struck twelve.'

In this key section, Scrooge questions the Spirit about what he conceals beneath his gown. As you read about who is revealed, consider in what ways they are symbolic figures.

Key context

This passage brings together some of Dickens's key ideas about children, education and poverty – and also has a huge dramatic impact in terms of the narration.

2 The first thing that Scrooge notices under the cloak is something he thinks might be 'a claw'. What does the word 'claw' automatically bring to mind?

3 Look at the description of the children Want and Ignorance.

   a Create a mood board of the main adjectives used, leaving space around them to add explanations and connotations (pictures or words these adjectives bring to mind). For example:

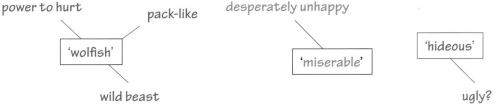

power to hurt

pack-like

desperately unhappy

'wolfish'

'miserable'

'hideous'

wild beast

ugly?

   b Colour-code the adjectives that are particularly likely to evoke emotions in the reader. Use one colour for sympathy or sadness and a second colour for disgust or fear.

4 Now take one or more similar adjectives from the passage and write about their effect on the reader. Consider how they link or contrast with earlier depictions of poverty (for example, Tiny Tim). One student, has written:

> The use of the word 'wolfish' is surprising; it suggests the children have the power to hurt or injure, like wild beasts. This is a rather different depiction of poverty than that represented by the kind, proud Cratchit family.

5 Why do you think Dickens withholds the appearance of Want and Ignorance until now, and why do they appear moments before the final Ghost?

6 Why do you think the Spirit suggests that Ignorance is to be feared more than Want?

Final task

Stave Three ends with the Spirit replying to Scrooge's question about whether there is any 'refuge' or 'resource' for the children Want and Ignorance.

7 What does the Spirit say? How does this link back to what Scrooge has said or done earlier in the novel?

End of chapter task

In these sets of lessons, you have looked at how, in *A Christmas Carol*, Dickens developed ideas about Christmas and poverty and its consequences, following on from the attitudes Scrooge expressed in Stave One.

Re-read this key extract from Stave Three and then complete the task that follows.

> The Grocers'! oh the Grocers'! nearly closed, with perhaps two shutters down, or one; but through those gaps such glimpses! It was not alone that the scales descending on the counter made a merry sound, or that the twine and roller parted company so briskly, or that the canisters were rattled up and down like juggling tricks, or even that the blended scents of tea and coffee were so grateful to the nose, or even that the raisins were so plentiful and rare, the almonds so extremely white, the sticks of cinnamon so long and straight, the other spices so delicious, the candied fruits so caked and spotted with molten sugar as to make the coldest lookers-on feel faint and subsequently bilious. Nor was it that the figs were moist and pulpy, or that the French plums blushed in modest tartness from their highly-decorated boxes, or that everything was good to eat and in its Christmas dress; but the customers were all so hurried and so eager in the hopeful promise of the day, that they tumbled up against each other at the door, crashing their wicker baskets wildly, and left their purchases upon the counter, and came running back to fetch them, and committed hundreds of the like mistakes, in the best humour possible; while the Grocer and his people were so frank and fresh that the polished hearts with which they fastened their aprons behind might have been their own, worn outside for general inspection, and for Christmas **daws** to peck at if they chose.

 1 Starting with this extract, write about the vision of Christmas that Dickens presents in *A Christmas Carol*. Write about:
- how he presents Christmas in this extract
- how he presents Christmas before this point in the text.

Glossary

daw: shortened form of term jackdaw, a bird that is supposed to steal precious things

Check your progress

- I can explain my ideas clearly in response to both shorter extracts and the text more widely.
- I understand the main methods Dickens used to present ideas.

- I can explain and develop my ideas thoughtfully in reference to both shorter extracts and the whole text.
- I can analyse a wide range of methods Dickens used to convey his ideas.

Chapter 5

Stave Four: Death and the city

English Literature

You will read:

- the first half of Stave Four of *A Christmas Carol.*

You will explore:

- ideas about the function of the Ghost of Christmas Yet to Come
- alternative depictions of the city of London and its poor.

English Language

You will read:

- Dickens's non-fiction accounts of his visit to a workhouse and a walk in London
- a student's descriptive account based on an image of Victorian London.

You will explore:

- how creative language features can be used in non-fiction texts
- how you can make your descriptive writing memorable.

How writers use language for effect for Paper 2 Question 3

Assessment objective
• AO2

How do writers achieve effects in non-fiction texts?

Writing about language in non-fiction texts

Remember that non-fiction writers often use many of the same language devices in their writing as you would find in fiction.

1 Read the following descriptions by Dickens. Can you tell which one is from *A Christmas Carol* and which is from a non-fiction account of walking in London?

> …streets of dirty, straggling houses… composed of buildings as ill-proportioned and deformed as the half-naked children that wallow in the kennels.

> The ways were foul and narrow; the shops and houses wretched; the people half-naked, drunken, slipshod, ugly.

2 Notice how both texts use a literary device – **personification** – to describe the buildings.

   a Find the words or phrases in each description that use personification.

   b What is the effect of this, in both cases?

To explore further, look closely at the particular words and phrases and their **connotations**. For example, what does describing the buildings as 'deformed' suggest about them? One student has made these notes:

> 'deformed' – unwell, misshapen, broken, diseased

3 Write down any connotations that come to mind from the following words:

   • wretched   • straggling   • foul.

Other language features and devices in non-fiction texts

Look out for other language features in non-fiction texts that you might associate with creative writing. Consider these examples from *A Christmas Carol*.

Key terms

personification: describing a natural feature (for example, a mountain) or an inanimate object (for example, a building) as though it has human characteristics

connotations: ideas, pictures or associations brought to mind

Type of language feature	Description/definition	Example
simile	comparing one thing to another	'Marley's face...like a bad lobster in a dark cellar' (Stave One)
metaphor	describing one thing as though it really is something else	'the houses opposite were mere phantoms' (Stave One)
assonance	repeating similar vowel sounds in a phrase or sentence OR: using identical consonants with different vowels	'Fowls clucked and strutted...' (Stave Two) 'anyhow and everyhow' (Stave Two)
alliteration	repeating the same sounds at the start of words in a phrase or sentence	'the setting sun had left a streak of fiery red' (Stave Three)
onomatopoeia	when the sound of a word matches the action or thing it describes	'shaggy ponies...trotting'; 'a squeak and scuffle from the mice' (Stave Two)

4 Which of these language features can you identify in this extract from a non-fiction account of Dickens's visit to a workhouse?

> In another room, were several ugly old women crouching, witch-like, round a hearth, and chattering and nodding, after the manner of the monkeys. 'All well here? And enough to eat?' A general chattering and chuckling; at last an answer from a volunteer. 'Oh yes, gentleman! Bless you, gentleman! Lord bless the Parish of St So-and-So!'
>
> From an article titled 'A Walk in a Workhouse', published in *Household Words* (1850)

5 Choose one of the language devices you have identified and explain its effect. What does it make you feel or think?

Combining language effects

When exploring the language in non-fiction texts, it is also important to explain how different word choices and language features combine to create an overall mood, or sense of a place or person.

6 Look again at the extract from Dickens's account of his visit to a workhouse. What is the overall effect Dickens wishes to convey about the women? Try to:

- pick out the specific words, phrases, sounds or patterns you notice
- consider their connotations – what they bring to mind.

Putting what you have learned into practice

Now you are ready to use what you have learned to analyse language choices in an unfamiliar non-fiction text.

The first writing that Dickens published professionally was a series of 'sketches' based on his walks around London and his observations of the characters he met there. In the following text, he describes a traveller entering the area known as 'Seven Dials' in London.

> He traverses streets of dirty, straggling houses, with now and then an unexpected court composed of buildings as ill-proportioned and deformed as the half-naked children that wallow in the kennels. Here and there, a little dark chandler's shop, with a cracked bell hung up behind the door to announce the entrance of a customer, or betray the presence of some young gentleman in whom a passion for shop tills has developed itself at an early age: others, as if for support, against some handsome lofty building, which **usurps** the place of a low dingy public-house; long rows of broken and patched windows expose plants that may have flourished when 'the Dials' were built, in vessels as dirty as 'the Dials' themselves; and shops for the purchase of rags, bones, old iron, and kitchen-stuff, vie in cleanliness with the bird-fanciers and rabbit-dealers, which one might fancy so many arks, but for the irresistible conviction that no bird in its proper senses, who was permitted to leave one of them, would ever come back again.
>
> Brokers' shops, which would seem to have been established by humane individuals, as refuges for destitute bugs, interspersed with announcements of day-schools, penny theatres, petition-writers, **mangles**, and music for balls or routs, complete the 'still life' of the subject; and dirty men, filthy women, squalid children, fluttering shuttlecocks, noisy **battledores**, reeking pipes, bad fruit, more than doubtful oysters, **attenuated** cats, depressed dogs, and anatomical fowls, are its cheerful accompaniments.
>
> From Dickens's *Sketches by Boz*, published between 1833 and 1836

Glossary

usurps: aggressively takes the place of

mangles: laundry machines with rollers for pressing or drying linen

battledore: a game similar to badminton

attenuated: weakened or extremely thin

SEVEN DIALS. (*From an Original*

At the end of this unit, you will complete an exam-style task on how Dickens uses language to describe the people and places around Seven Dials.

7 To prepare for the final task, start by focusing on *specific words or phrases* in the extract that tell the reader about the people and places in Seven Dials.

- Look for references to: men, women, children, shops, buildings, streets.

- 'Zoom in' on particular words and analyse their connotations and effects. For example, 'reeking' does not just mean 'slightly smelly'.

Copy and complete a table like the one below.

How they are described – particular words or phrases chosen	Language form or device	The effect: what it suggests about the people or places
'dirty men' and 'filthy women' 'refuges for destitute bugs'	noun phrases	Suggest grimy people and places – it's a safe place for fleas and other insects to thrive!

For higher marks, you need to explain the overall tone or mood of the extract. For example, look at the phrase:

> Brokers' shops, which would seem to have been established by humane individuals, as refuges for destitute bugs…

Taken at face value, this means 'shops set up by kind individuals as places of safety for homeless bugs'. However, it is likely Dickens is being **ironic** or slightly humorous. So, a suitable analysis would be:

Key terms

ironic: creating a comic or knowing tone at odds with the apparent meaning of a statement

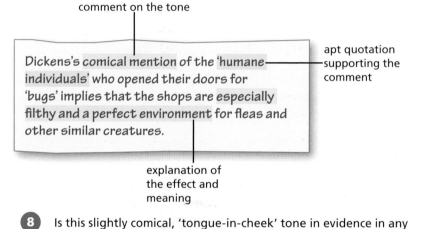

comment on the tone

Dickens's comical mention of the 'humane individuals' who opened their doors for 'bugs' implies that the shops are especially filthy and a perfect environment for fleas and other similar creatures.

apt quotation supporting the comment

explanation of the effect and meaning

 8 Is this slightly comical, 'tongue-in-cheek' tone in evidence in any of the other examples from the Seven Dials text? If so, add this to your table.

Checklist for success

✔ Select no more than 3 or 4 language choices or features.

✔ Comment on the connotations of individual words and phrases and the effects created.

✔ Comment on the overall tone or mood created.

Final task

9 Now complete this exam-style task.

Refer to Dickens's account of Seven Dials.
How does Dickens use language to describe the people and places? **[12 marks]**

Introducing the Ghost of Christmas Yet to Come

Assessment objectives
• AO1, AO2, AO3

> ### How does Dickens present the Ghost of Christmas Yet to Come?

Death in Victorian England

Death and **mortality** are central concerns of *A Christmas Carol*. Given the mortality rates in Victorian England, this is hardly surprising.

1 Look at the graph of English life expectancy, 1840–1935.

    a What was the average life expectancy in 1843 (when *A Christmas Carol* was published)?

    b As this is an average, what do you think life expectancy was for poorer working-class people?

2 In the poorer quarters of Britain's larger cities, a child born in the 1830s and 1840s had a one in five (20 per cent) chance of dying by their fifth birthday.

    How do you think this childhood mortality rate would have affected readers of *A Christmas Carol* in Dickens's day?

Analysing the Third Ghost more closely

Dickens introduces the final Ghost at the end of Stave Three:

> Scrooge…beheld a solemn Phantom, draped and hooded, coming, like a mist along the ground, towards him.

Key terms

mortality: the fact that you will die eventually; also the frequency of death in a population

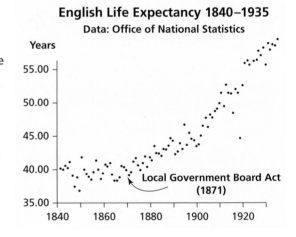

English Life Expectancy 1840–1935
Data: Office of National Statistics

Years

Local Government Board Act (1871)

3 What are your immediate impressions of the Third Ghost? Make notes.

Most readers in both Dickens's time and today would immediately link the appearance of the Third Ghost with that of the **Grim Reaper**. It raises the question about who the Reaper's scythe will fall on: will it be Scrooge, to punish him for his past behaviour, or, as predicted, Tiny Tim – vulnerable as so many poor or sick Victorian children were?

Key terms

Grim Reaper: personification of death; a tall skeletal figure, shrouded in black and carrying a scythe, who collects the souls of the recently dead and takes them to the afterlife

4 **a** Create a 'quotation board' about the Third Ghost, like the one below, based on the section of Stave Four you have read so far.

'draped and hooded'

'coming, like a mist along the ground,'

'difficult to…separate from the darkness'

Find quotations, to add to the ones above, about:
- how the Ghost looks and behaves
- how Scrooge reacts to the Ghost.

b Look carefully at the quotations you have selected. What does each one reveal about the Ghost? How do the quotations tie in with the idea of mortality or impending death?

One student has turned his thoughts into an explanatory paragraph:

selected quotation

Dickens describes the ghost 'coming, like a mist along the ground,' towards Scrooge. The simile 'like a mist' creates a gothic and sinister mood, and also suggests the Ghost is going to overpower him in the way that death can come at any time and any moment.

explains the tone/mood created

language device

offers a second interpretation

c Choose a quotation of your own about the Third Ghost and write an analysis of it in a similar way.

5 How does the final Ghost compare with the previous one? You could make parallel 'quotation boards' for them and/or create a simple table like the one below.

Feature	Ghost of Christmas Present	Ghost of Christmas Yet to Come
physical appearance	'jolly Giant'; 'genial face'	
actions	Takes Scrooge through streets at Christmas… Takes Scrooge to…	
speech		
symbolic impact	Life, kindness and…	

Final task

 6 Write a paragraph about your overall impressions of the Ghost of Christmas Yet to Come. Comment on:
- the Ghost's appearance, speech and behaviour
- the effect it has on Scrooge
- what it seems to represent or symbolise.

Corruption and poverty in the City

Assessment objectives
- AO1, AO3

Text references
You will have read from:
- 'They scarcely seemed to enter the city…' To 'My life tends that way, now.'

Why does the Ghost show Scrooge these final scenes?

In the first few pages of Stave Four, Scrooge meets the final Ghost and is horrified by its deathly presence. Next, the Ghost takes Scrooge to two locations in the city – first to the business district and then to the slums.

City business

In the first location, the ghost shows Scrooge's three men of business in conversation. Bearing in mind that Scrooge knows these men, anything Dickens says about them should be examined carefully. For example, Dickens describes the businessmen in the following ways:

- a man 'taking a vast quantity of snuff out of a very large snuff-box'
- 'a great fat man with a monstrous chin'
- a 'red-faced gentleman with a pendulous excrescence on the end of his nose'.

1 What is the overall impression of these three men from each description? Think about the adjectives 'vast', 'very large', 'great fat' and 'monstrous', and the noun 'excrescence' (growth). If you were to associate these men with one of the seven deadly sins, which one would it be?

2 It is clear to the reader (if not to Scrooge) who and what their subject is.

   a Why do you think Dickens does not allow Scrooge to guess they are discussing his own death? For example, what does it tell us about Scrooge and his readiness to change?

   b What is the dramatic effect of revealing Scrooge's death to the reader in this way?

Old Joe's

From here, Scrooge is surprised to find himself in another, poorer part of the city.

3 Look at the picture (right) by Gustave Doré. What can you see?

   a Who is in it? What (if anything) are they doing?

   b How would you describe their appearance?

4 What impression is given by the image of this part of London?

Now read the following extract from Stave Four, about the 'obscure part of the town' where Scrooge is taken.

> The ways were foul and narrow; the shops and houses wretched; the people half-naked, drunken, slipshod, ugly. Alleys and archways, like so many cesspools, disgorged their offences of smell, and dirt, and life, upon the straggling streets; and the whole quarter reeked with crime, with filth, and misery.
>
> Far in this den of infamous resort, there was a low-browed, beetling shop, below a pent-house roof, where iron, old rags, bottles, bones, and greasy offal, were bought. Upon the floor within, were piled up heaps of rusty keys, nails, chains, hinges, files, scales, weights, and refuse iron of all kinds. Secrets that few would like to scrutinise were bred and hidden in mountains of unseemly rags, masses of corrupted fat, and sepulchres of bones. Sitting in among the wares he dealt in, by a charcoal stove, made of old bricks, was a grey-haired rascal, nearly seventy years of age; who had screened himself from the cold air without, by a frousy curtaining of miscellaneous tatters, hung upon a line; and smoked his pipe in all the luxury of calm retirement.

5 How does Dickens represent the poor and this part of the city here? Look at the highlighted sections.

  a How are the people described? What attitude does Dickens seem to have towards them?

  b How is the shop personified?

  c How does the 'mountains' of items here contrast with the mountain of food in Stave Three?

6 What symbolic child-figures from Stave Three are you reminded of in the first paragraph above? How are they similar?

7 In what way does the description of Old Joe's contrast with that of the Cratchits' home?

8 Shortly after this, we find out why the three people at Old Joe's have met.

  a What are they discussing?

  b Why does Scrooge find it particularly repellent and shocking?

Final task

Make sure you have read up until the point when Scrooge leaves the slums ('My life tends that way, now').

9 Write two paragraphs about why the Ghost chooses to show Scrooge these final visions of the city – both the corrupted rich and poor. Consider:

  • how the descriptions of the City businessmen convey ideas about corruption and moral decay

  • how the depiction of the area around Old Joe's contrasts or links with earlier portrayals of poverty and its effects.

Descriptive writing: dark places for Paper 1 Question 5

Assessment objectives
- AO5, AO6

How can you make your descriptive writing memorable?

When writing to describe, it is worth taking a few lessons from Dickens himself. He is a master of creating vivid, powerful pictures that convey a particular tone or mood.

For example, imagine Dickens had been asked to write a description to accompany the engraving below, by Gustave Doré. How would he have approached it?

Engraving of the slums of London by Gustave Doré.

Being specific

1. What is lacking in this descriptive sentence? Would Dickens have been happy with it?

> The smoke covered the building.

This description leaves the reader with an imprecise picture of a scene. Lots of questions remain unanswered:

- What *sort* of building?
- *How* was it 'covered'?
- *What* was the smoke like?

A better description might be:

> The house was cloaked by the smoke.

This specifies the type of building, and the metaphorical use of the verb 'cloak' creates an interesting picture of the shape of the smoke. However, the description could still be better.

Using the senses

To improve the description, you could draw on the five senses to convey the atmosphere of the picture. You could add appropriate adjectives to convey:

- the shape or style of the house

> detached
> grand
> airy
> looming
> narrow

- the colour of the smoke
- the smell, or even the taste, of the smoke.

2 Copy and complete this sentence:

> The .... house was cloaked by the
> .... smoke.

Controlling the focus

You also need to structure your description so that you control what the reader sees. Think about:

- the *order* of view (what is seen first, then next, and so on)
- the *choice* of focus (will you start with a small detail and zoom outwards?).

As a descriptive writer, it can be useful to think of yourself as operating a video camera, with the ability to zoom in, out, pan up and down across a scene – even stop, and select a new shot.

For example, consider this student's description of the Doré engraving.

> A pale waxy light pervaded the curving tail of the backyards that stretched away into the gloomy distance. Behind a washing line strung limply across a courtyard, a gaunt man sat slumped forward, staring into the dregs of an empty mug with a chipped edge. The brim of his hat cast a thin, dark line over his forehead, like a trickle of dirt.

3 Trace the focus here:

a Which sentence establishes the general, long-shot of the scene?

b What – or who – is the focus at the start of the second sentence? How does the focus change after the comma?

c How does the focus shift again after the second comma in the second sentence?

d Which final detail in the last sentence makes the reader 'zoom in'?

Inventive imagery

Imagery features strongly in the descriptions above. It can be one way to make your writing inventive and engaging. For example, **personification** is used in the example of the 'curving tail of the backyards'. **Simile** and **metaphor** are also key ways of reimagining scenes or people.

4 How is simile used at the end of the final sentence? Why is this an apt comparison, given the scene?

Key terms

personification: a personification of something abstract is its representation in the form of a person

simile: an expression which describes a person or thing as being similar to someone or something else

metaphor: an imaginative way of describing something by referring to something else which is the same in a particular way

Final task

5 Now complete this exam-style task.

Write your own description based on the sketch by Gustave Doré on the page opposite.

(24 marks for content and organisation

16 marks for technical accuracy)

[40 marks]

Checklist for success

✔ **Begin** by generating as much **specific vocabulary** about the scene as possible. Start with what can be seen – but also use your imagination to consider what could be there, even if not actually visible.

✔ Start with a description of the **whole scene** and then '**zoom in**' on specific items, details or movements.

✔ Try to convey an **overall idea or mood** through the description and your use of imagery.

End of chapter task

Read this extract from Stave Four. In it, Scrooge listens to Mrs Dilber talk about how she stole a good-quality calico shirt from a corpse.

> 'What do you call wasting of it?' asked old Joe.
>
> 'Putting it on him to be buried in, to be sure,' replied the woman with a laugh. 'Somebody was fool enough to do it, but I took it off again. If calico an't good enough for such a purpose, it isn't good enough for anything. It's quite as becoming to the body. He can't look uglier than he did in that one.'
>
> Scrooge listened to this dialogue in horror. As they sat grouped about their spoil, in the scanty light afforded by the old man's lamp, he viewed them with a detestation and disgust, which could hardly have been greater, though they had been obscene demons, marketing the corpse itself.

Write two paragraphs.

- In the first, explain what this scene has to say about the theme of money/business.
- In the second, explain how Dickens presents the people in the slums through Scrooge's eyes.

Check your progress

- I can explain my ideas clearly about the functions of characters and settings.
- I understand the main methods Dickens used to present ideas.

- I can explain and develop my ideas thoughtfully about the functions of characters and settings.
- I can analyse a wide range of methods that Dickens used to present ideas.

Stave Four: Narrative matters

English Literature

You will read:

- Stave Four of *A Christmas Carol*.

You will explore:

- the function of the corpse and debtor family scenes
- the function, impact on the reader and thematic importance of the death of Tiny Tim
- how Dickens explores the theme of kindness
- different interpretations of the dramatic climax of the novel
- how Dickens presents Scrooge's repentance.

English Language

You will read:

- extracts from a student's own story.

You will explore:

- story structure
- how to write stories that are memorable and interesting for the reader.

Facing up to responsibility

Assessment objectives
- AO2, AO3

Text references
You will have read from:
- 'Merciful Heaven, what is this!' to '…was one of pleasure'.

What is the function of the corpse and debtor family scenes?

The two scenes Scrooge now witnesses seem, at first glance, to be unconnected. In the first, Scrooge finds himself in a room with a corpse; in the second, he witnesses a family scene related to debt. What are the functions of these key scenes?

Writing about a key scene

When exploring the function of a key scene, it is important to establish the context – what has just happened, and its place in the overall structure of the book.

Read what one student has written about the first part of Stave Four and the section starting 'Merciful Heaven…' and ending 'I have not the power.'

> Key term
>
> **dramatic irony:** the tension created when the audience or reader knows more about a situation than the character does

In the first part of Stave Four, the Ghost has shown Scrooge two scenes – one with his former business colleagues, and one with 'demons' from the slums, discussing a corpse. In each case, we as readers, but not Scrooge, realise the dead man is Scrooge himself. Dickens now develops this dramatic irony even more by placing Scrooge close to his own corpse in a moment of intense tension.

— explains the immediate context of the scene

— explains one aspect of the function of the scene – to build drama

1 Think about how the 'corpse scene' links, not just to what has just happened in Stave Four, but to the novel *as a whole*. What different 'versions' of Scrooge have we seen?

Copy and complete this table. You could add who – or what – have been Scrooge's companions at these times.

Version 1: *Scrooge as an old, grumpy businessman*	Companion/s: *memory of Marley; Bob*
Version 2: *Scrooge as a school boy*	Companion/s: *no one, until Fan 'rescues' him*
Version 3:	Companion/s:
Version 4:	Companion/s:
Version 5: *Scrooge as a corpse*	Companion/s:

2 What are Scrooge's reactions to seeing the corpse? Select three or four key words or phrases that tell the reader about his state of mind at this point. For example:

> 'He recoiled in terror' – Scrooge is in a dark room with a corpse that he almost touches – no wonder he is afraid. The verb 'recoiled' means he is physically revolted and turns away, but the ghost makes him face the table.

3 Now write your own paragraph about the function of the 'corpse scene'. Use these prompts and add in any appropriate quotation from the section:

> - Scrooge viewing his own corpse is a logical conclusion to events, as we have already seen...
> - The scene creates a powerful message about the consequences of selfishness, as Scrooge describes the corpse as...

The debtor's family

As the 'corpse' scene ends, Scrooge asks to be shown anyone who 'feels emotion caused by this man's death'. The Spirit now takes Scrooge to visit a family.

◆ Read from 'If there is any person in the town...' to 'was one of pleasure'.

4 What do you think Scrooge is hoping for when he asks to see anyone who 'feels emotion'?

5 Make notes about:
- how the mother behaves before the husband arrives
- how the husband is described when he appears (his face, expression)
- how both react to the news that their 'creditor' is dead.

Final task

6 Write a paragraph exploring the function of the scene with the debtor's family.

Checklist for success

✔ Include the immediate context – what has come just before it, and why this is relevant/linked to it.

✔ Consider the scene in the wider context of the whole novel. How does it link, if at all, to other scenes?

✔ Ensure you focus on the scene itself and make detailed reference to language and ideas.

Tiny Tim and the theme of kindness

Assessment objectives
- AO1, AO2

Text references
You will have read from:
- 'Let me see some tenderness…' to '…thy childish essence was from God!'

How does Dickens explore the theme of kindness in this scene?

When Scrooge asked, in the previous scene, to witness some 'emotion' over the dead man, what he sees from the debtor and his wife is happiness and relief at the death. This time Scrooge adapts his question and asks: 'Let me see some tenderness connected with a death.' He still holds out some hope that the dead man – awful though he was – inspired some love or kindness. But, yet again, what the Third Ghost shows Scrooge brings little relief.

How are the Cratchits presented?

What evidence is there of the Cratchit family's kindness and dignity in the face of Tiny Tim's death? Consider these extracts from this section:

> - 'Quiet. Very quiet. The noisy little Cratchits were still as statues in one corner.'
> - 'His [Bob's] tea was ready for him on the hob, and they all tried who should help him to it most.'
> - 'Then the two young Cratchits got upon his knees and laid, each child a little cheek, against his face.'

1 Take each extract in turn, and explain the effect of particular details on how we view the Cratchit family. For example, why is the observation that the children were 'still as statues' so moving?

2 When Bob goes upstairs, Dickens says:

> Poor Bob sat down in the chair and when he had thought a little and composed himself, he kissed the little face. He was reconciled to what had happened, and went down again quite happy.

The word 'happy' is used to describe Bob here – and he is also described as being 'cheerful' with the children. Mrs Cratchit speaks in a 'cheerful voice' about Bob carrying Tim home. What point do you think Dickens is making about the Cratchit family by using this word?

Key context

There is a convention in ghost stories of supernatural forces wilfully twisting what a mortal person says. For example, in 'The Monkey's Paw' by W.W. Jacobs, a family is granted three wishes. Their first wish is for money to pay off a loan – they get it, but it is in the form of financial compensation, after their son is killed in a factory accident. Each wish brings something more terrible.

The kindness of others

Bob then describes Fred's 'extraordinary kindness' and how he was 'heartily sorry', and how he offered his services to Bob and gave him his card. Bob says:

> 'It really seemed as if he had known our Tiny Tim, and felt with us' … 'I shouldn't be at all surprised – mark what I say! – if he got Peter a better situation.'

We have seen kindness shown by characters previously, such as Fezziwig to his employees and Fan to the young Scrooge. Now we see it again in this scene. There are several ways you could incorporate analysis of the language above into an exploration of the theme of kindness. For example:

- you could simply explain what it tells us about Fred, given his lack of actual connection to the Cratchits
- you could comment on the difference between Scrooge and Fred, and how these words emphasise this
- you could comment on wider ideas about kindness – for example, how people in the story so far have made it their 'business' to be responsible for others and show empathy for them, or how kindness links to Christian values through the description of Tiny Tim.

You could even combine all three approaches!

 One student has made a start. Complete their paragraph by developing their exploration of the theme of kindness.

> Bob comments that it seemed Fred 'had known' Tiny Tim and felt his death 'with us'. This demonstrates that you do not have to be personally connected to the person who has died in order to feel sympathy for another's loss. Kindness is also shown in Bob's belief that Fred might give…

Final task

4 Now write a paragraph analysing the effect of Tiny Tim's death and memory on both the Cratchit family, Scrooge and the reader. You could consider:

- what Bob says in the extract below about Tim's character
- Dickens's final words in this section: 'thy childish essence was from God!'
- what Dickens makes us feel about death and its effect on others (especially compared with previous scenes, such as the one with the coffin or at old Joe's).

> 'And I know,' said Bob, 'I know, my dears, that when we recollect how patient and how mild he was; although he was a little, little child; we shall not quarrel easily among ourselves, and forget poor Tiny Tim in doing it.'

A dramatic climax: interpreting Scrooge's repentance

Assessment objectives
• AO1, AO2

Text references
You will have read from:
• '"Spectre," said Scrooge, "something informs me…"' to the end of the Stave.

How does Dickens present Scrooge's repentance?

Scrooge has been on a journey both literal (in terms of time and places) and spiritual. This next section of the book represents the dramatic climax, when we see whether or not he has learned the lessons of the journey.

Interpreting Scrooge

Interpretation is the ability to look at information or ideas in a text and explore possible explanations for them. This sort of thoughtful reflection is an important aspect of higher attainment at GCSE.

For example, a key 'problem' occurs in this Stave – Scrooge fails to realise that he is the dead person. What possible reasons are there for this? One student has written:

> Dickens's only reason for presenting Scrooge as ignorant about his own death is that it makes the scenes when he is with the corpse or when he sees the young family more dramatic and tense.

1 Do you agree with this interpretation? Or is there more to Dickens's intentions as an author here?

The table below shows some other possible interpretations. Copy and complete the table, adding comments and supporting evidence of your own.

Interpretation	Supporting evidence
A: Scrooge hasn't really changed yet. He isn't fully able to confront his guilt.	*Scrooge was so self-centred at the start, and has been alone so he has little self-awareness, yet…*
B: Scrooge *does* know – deep down. His questions and comments show this.	
C: Scrooge is absolutely terrified. His fear means he cannot think properly.	
Your own interpretation:	

Interpreting Scrooge's transformation

◆ Read from 'Before I draw nearer to that stone…' to 'The kind hand trembled.'

2 At the end of this section, Scrooge says, 'I am not the man I was.' How do you interpret this statement from what he says and does here? Make notes about:

a any *questions* which show Scrooge finally working things out for himself

b the *gestures and movements* Scrooge makes (for example, 'crept towards it' and 'cried, upon his knees'), and what this tells us about his state of mind

c *what Scrooge says* in the section where he cries, 'hear me!' and *why* it might have made the Spirit's hand 'shake' for the first time.

Now read Scrooge's final, important speech of this Stave:

'I will honour Christmas in my heart, and try to keep it all the year. I will live in the Past, the Present, and the Future. The Spirits of all Three shall strive within me. I will not shut out the lessons that they teach. Oh, tell me I may sponge away the writing on this stone!'

In his agony, he caught the spectral hand. It sought to free itself, but he was strong in his entreaty, and detained it. The Spirit, stronger yet, repulsed him.

Holding up his hands in a last prayer to have his fate reversed, he saw an alteration in the Phantom's hood and dress. It shrunk, collapsed, and dwindled down into a bedpost.

---

3 a What simple verb after 'I' does Scrooge use three times in the first paragraph here? What does this suggest about his intentions (how committed he sounds)?

b What final action or gesture does Scrooge make which signals his commitment to change?

Final task

4 Now write up your notes in a longer response of two or three paragraphs, interpreting the depth of Scrooge's transformation and repentance.

Checklist for success

✔ Explore interpretations of the words 'transformation' and 'repentance'. What *sort* of change has Scrooge undergone, and how does Dickens present it?

✔ Comment on Scrooge's inability (until right at the end) to recognise the dead body as his own and your interpretation of why this might be.

✔ Select quotations carefully from this section as evidence.

Narrative writing for Paper 1 Question 5

Assessment objectives
- AO5, AO6

How can I make my stories memorable and interesting for the reader?

If you were to sum up the qualities that make up a good story, they would probably include:

- an interesting *plot* or *narrative* that makes the reader want to know what happens next
- a compelling, believable *main character*
- vivid *settings* that the reader can easily picture
- *dialogue* that adds to our understanding of character and events.

Stage One: plan your narrative

Imagine you have been set the task to write the opening to a story in which a powerful event or surprising moment changes someone's life for the better. Stories are sometimes described as having five stages:

1. Introduction	2. Rising action	3. Climax	4. Falling action	5. Conclusion
Main character, setting or situation introduced	Drama builds, problems emerge	Moment of highest drama or emotion	Tension lessens	Issues and problems revealed or resolved

 1 Can you fit the events of *A Christmas Carol* in to these five stages?

2 Now, can you come up with your own story structure based on the task? (Even if the task specifies the opening, you need to know where your story is going.)

Stage Two: make your opening compelling

A Christmas Carol begins with the mysterious, riddle-like phrase 'Marley was dead to begin with.'

This:

- captures our imagination by raising the question 'If he was dead to begin with, what is he *now?*'
- on a simpler level also raises the question 'Who is Marley?'
- has an immediate, dramatic impact through its shortness and directness.

Some openings go a stage further in terms of withholding information and making the reader ask questions. Here is one student's opening sentence.

Who is this? What is this?

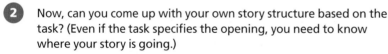

When she opened it, the light poured in. She stood staring out, glad that the suffocating air was dispersing. —————— Why is the air like this?

3 Write the next sentence of this opening paragraph, perhaps naming who the person is and what she is opening.

Stage Three: establish a powerful setting

Choose a few vivid details to create an immediate atmosphere or to advance the storyline. Consider this next part of the student's story:

> The dark walls [1] were hung with dusty paintings of Alice's ancestors. [1] Her grandfather's ancient desk [1] dominated the room, but it was the sheaf of papers on the scratched mahogany surface [1] that drew her eye: his will. [2]

4 What sort of atmosphere do the noun phrases numbered [1] convey?

5 How do the setting and the final noun [2] suggest a storyline?

6 Add a further two sentences, maintaining the same mood but also revealing more of the plot.

Stage Four: introduce engaging characters

Make sure your main character is distinctive. You can achieve this through the same 'people pointers' applied to the characterisation of Scrooge (see Lesson 2.2 on pages 24–25):

7 How effectively has the same student done this in the example below? Which of the characterisation pointers have been used?

> She almost retched: the place was disgusting. Alice sneered. Did she care about her grandfather's lonely old death? She took out her mobile and texted Lee. 'Come over here now. N keep your mouth shut ok.' Her screen reflected her almost bald scalp for a moment, and in a fit of rage she flung the phone across the room.

8 Spend five minutes planning who your central character is, and how they are connected to the powerful event. Jot down details about their looks, behaviour, age, and so on. Get a clear idea in your mind.

Final task

9 Now complete this exam-style task.

> Write the opening part of a story in which a powerful event or surprising moment changes someone's life for better or worse.
>
> (24 marks for content and organisation
> 16 marks for technical accuracy)
>
> **[40 marks]**

Checklist for success

✔ Make your story compelling in the ways suggested.

✔ Check your technical accuracy (spelling, punctuation and grammar) – they are worth 40 per cent of your marks!

End of chapter task

You have seen in Stave Four how Dickens takes Scrooge to the depths of despair before he finally achieves his moment of self-realisation. So why does this process take so long?

 1 Re-read the following extract from the section in Stave Four, when Scrooge sees the corpse of a man in a room. Then complete the task that follows.

He thought, if this man could be raised up now, what would be his foremost thoughts? Avarice, hard-dealing, griping cares? They have brought him to a rich end, truly!

He lay, in the dark empty house, with not a man, a woman, or a child to say he was kind to me in this or that, and for the memory of one kind word I will be kind to him. A cat was tearing at the door, and there was a sound of gnawing rats beneath the hearth-stone. What *they* wanted in the room of death, and why they were so restless and disturbed, Scrooge did not dare to think.

'Spirit!' he said, 'this is a fearful place. In leaving it, I shall not leave its lesson, trust me. Let us go!'

Still the Ghost pointed with an unmoved finger to the head.

'I understand you,' Scrooge returned, 'and I would do it, if I could. But I have not the power, Spirit. I have not the power.'

Again it seemed to look upon him.

 2 Starting with this extract, how does Dickens present the idea of the importance of true repentance in *A Christmas Carol*?

Write about:

- how Dickens presents Scrooge's understanding of his actions at this point in the novel
- how Dickens presents Scrooge's understanding of his actions at other times in the text.

Check your progress

- I can explain my ideas about narrative structure clearly in response to shorter extracts and the text more widely.
- I understand the main methods Dickens uses to present ideas.

- I can explain and develop my ideas thoughtfully about narrative structure in reference to shorter extracts and the whole text.
- I can analyse a wide range of methods Dickens uses to convey his ideas.

Stave Five: Full circle

English Literature

You will read:

- Stave Five of *A Christmas Carol*.

You will explore:

- how Dickens present Scrooge's rebirth and redemption
- how to write effective analytical paragraphs about Dickens's use of language
- how to write about structural ideas across a whole text.

English Language

You will read:

- two newspaper articles on homelessness at Christmas – one from 1845 and one from 2013.

You will explore:

- how to identify and comment on viewpoints in two unfamiliar texts
- how to write an article in which you express your views about festive holidays.

How Dickens presents the new Scrooge

Assessment objectives
- AO1, AO2

Text references
You will have read from:
- 'Yes! and the bedpost was his own…' to 'Glorious!'

How does Dickens present Scrooge's rebirth?

At the end of the Stave Four, we saw Scrooge at his lowest point emotionally – a broken man, begging for the chance to **atone**. Once the Third Ghost disappears, Dickens presents a 'new' Scrooge in a range of different ways.

Key term

atone: originally a religious term meaning to make up for something bad or sinful you have done

How Dickens uses language to show Scrooge's transformation

It is important to construct thoughtful analytical passages about characters. To do this, you need to examine specific examples of Dickens's use of language to describe Scrooge. For example, consider this bank of quotations about Scrooge's actions taken from the section.

Quotation bank

'he scrambled out of bed'	'his broken voice'	'his face was wet with tears'
'his hands were busy with his garments… putting them on upside down, tearing them, mislaying them…'	'laughing and crying in the same breath' 'he had… frisked into the sitting-room…'	'it was a splendid laugh, a most illustrious laugh'

 Select one or two quotations and jot down notes about the key words or phrases, explaining what they suggest and what we learn about Scrooge from them. For example, 'scrambled' suggests a hurried, almost desperate action – as though Scrooge realises there is no time to lose.

You can use the adjective bank below if it helps, or create your own.

Adjective bank

emotional	desperate	active	passive	hurried	panicking
overwhelmed	comical	ridiculous	ecstatic	anxious	light-hearted

 Scrooge also says a great deal in this scene – and most of it to himself.

a What is notable about what he says and how he says it? (Think about the length of sentences, the punctuation, any repetition.)

b Why does Dickens have Scrooge speak his thoughts *aloud*, rather than simply present them as thoughts? (Think about Scrooge's state of mind, and how keen he is to check that what he sees is real.)

What imagery does Dickens use to convey Scrooge's rebirth?

◆ Re-read Scrooge's speech about himself from 'I don't know what to do...' to 'Hallo! Whoop! Hallo here!'

It would be easy to pass over this section as a fairly comical and lively account of Scrooge's transformation. However, it is worth considering why Dickens selected these four particular similes. Consider the connotations in each case.

For example, the student's notes below show that being 'as light as a feather' has two types of possible meaning – physical and also emotional.

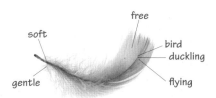

soft
free
gentle
bird
duckling
flying

 3 Take each of the remaining similes and make notes in a similar way.

Now read this student's analysis based on the notes:

> Scrooge describes himself as being 'as light as a feather'. This is significant because it gives a sense of Scrooge's physical change; rather than the slow-moving, methodical man of the start of the novel, now he is leaping around without a care in the world. However, it also suggests Scrooge no longer carries the burdens of his old life – his greed and obsession with business. It is significant that Marley was weighed down by cash-boxes, chains and padlocks. So was Scrooge, emotionally, but now he is liberated.

4 How is this an effective analytical paragraph?

   a Where does this response draw a contrast between two different Scrooges? What is the point made?

   b What alternative interpretation of the word 'light' is made?

   c How is this point emphasised by reference to Marley?

   d What overall point is made in the final summing-up sentence?

Final task

 5 Take any one of the similes and write a paragraph like the one in the example.

Remember to:

- look at any wider or inferred meanings
- try to link the simile and your interpretation with other events in the text.

Making amends: from Stave One to Five

Assessment objectives
- AO1, AO2

Text references
You will have read from:
- 'Running to the window…' to the end of the Stave.

How does Dickens use the final Stave to bring Scrooge's redemption full circle?

The next part of Stave Five is also full of activity, and continues the idea of a renewed Scrooge. In particular, it develops the structural idea of mirroring between Staves One and Five.

Exploring links between Stave Five and Stave One

One passage in Stave Five describes how Scrooge, while walking the streets:

> patted the children on the head, and questioned beggars, and looked down into the kitchens of houses…

1 How does this passage contrast with the manner in which Scrooge returned from work in Stave One? Write a simple paragraph comparing the two.

2 In Stave Five, Scrooge acts in significant ways to address the wrongs from Stave One.

For each action he takes, make notes in a table like the one below, to describe:

- how each shows him making amends, or indicates a significant change in his character
- how each links back to, or mirrors, similar events in Stave One.

Scrooge's actions in Stave Five	Links with Stave One (what is Scrooge amending?)
Meets and speaks to a 'loitering' boy about the turkey for sale in the shop	
Speaks pleasantly to the knocker on his door in friendly and grateful terms…	Shocked by the change in the knocker's 'livid colour' when transformed into the face of Marley. Has a 'terrible sensation'.
Meets the charity collectors in the street and…	
Visits Fred, his nephew, and…	
Gets into work early on Boxing Day, and speaks to Bob when he arrives…	

3 For each moment you identified in Question 2, write a paragraph in which you:

- describe Scrooge's *original behaviour/attitude* from Stave One, stating what it tells us and supported with an appropriate quotation
- explain how *things are now* in Stave Five and what this reveals about Scrooge, supported with an appropriate quotation.

For example, a student has started writing about the knocker on the door:

> Scrooge's initial reaction in Stave One to the face of Marley on his knocker is one of shock and unpleasantness. We are told its 'livid colour made it horrible' and Scrooge was 'conscious of a terrible sensation'. Scrooge is unsettled by it, despite his fierce and hard exterior. However, when he sees the door knocker in the final Stave, his reaction is in complete contrast. He…

Complete the student's paragraph and then complete each of the others. Use structural vocabulary such as: 'at first/earlier in the novel', 'now', 'yet', 'in contrast', 'in this/that case', 'at that time', 'on this occasion', 'originally'.

Happy ever after

◆ Read the final two paragraphs of Stave Five, from 'Scrooge was better than his word' to the end.

Write down your thoughts in response to each of these questions.

4 What is the significance of the simple statement '…and to Tiny Tim, who did *not* die, he was a second father'? Consider:

- Why is it vital to Dickens's message that Tim survives?
- Given what we know of Scrooge's past, why might readers be moved by the reference to him as a 'second father'?

5 **a** What adjective dominates the penultimate paragraph? (It is used seven times.) Why is this word made so prominent?

b Choose an adjective to sum up Scrooge from the *first* description of him in Stave One. Does it reveal how much he has changed?

6 Why do you think Dickens decides to give the final words of the story to Tiny Tim?

Final task

7 Write a paragraph to summarise the extent of the change in Scrooge in the final Stave of *A Christmas Carol*.

- Succinctly sum up the main changes between Scrooge in Stave One and Scrooge in Stave Five.
- Select at least one quotation that sums up both the 'old' Scrooge and the 'new' one.

Comparing viewpoints and perspectives for Paper 2 Question 4

Assessment objective
- AO3

· ·

> ### How do I approach a task that asks me to identify and comment on viewpoints in two unfamiliar texts?

In Paper 2 Question 4 of your GCSE English Language exam, you have to read and respond to two non-fiction sources. To some extent, you will have already looked for points of similarity or difference between the two sources as part of a summary/comprehension question (Paper 2 Question 2 – see Chapter 3, Lesson 4 on pages 38–43). However, in Question 4 you are being assessed on your ability to:

- find evidence of particular viewpoints – and explain what they are
- discuss how the writer gets their point of view across (the techniques they use)
- support your analysis with close reference to the text
- compare the particular perspectives of each writer.

What should you be looking for when comparing two non-fiction texts?

Each non-fiction source will be different, but as a guide, these features are worth checking for, especially when the texts express a personal viewpoint:

✔ reference to personal experience or **anecdotal** evidence (for example, 'One night, while I was working for a charity...')

✔ direct statements of belief, such as 'I think that...', 'It is wrong that...'

✔ **emotive** or loaded language or imagery (for example, 'It is totally unacceptable...', 'Desperate lines of starving people...')

✔ other **rhetorical** effects, such as sarcasm or irony, rhetorical questions, a range of sentences for effect (short, long, and so on)

✔ structural effects – the way a text builds an argument, or changes tack.

In the final task for this unit, you will compare how the writers of the following two texts have conveyed their different views about charitable giving or volunteering at Christmas.

1 Read the texts on pages 87 and 88. As you read the second text (the *Guardian* article), try to consider in what ways the perspective is similar to, or different from, the *Spectator* article.

Key terms

anecdotal: referring to brief, personal experience

emotive: evoking a strong feeling in the reader

rhetorical: designed to provoke a particular response in a reader, such as shock or amusement

Glossary

unction: strong expression of emotion (originally religious)

The following text is taken from an article from the *Spectator* newspaper. It was written in 1845, a couple of years after *A Christmas Carol*. In it, the writer discusses the habit of wealthy people sending Christmas dinner to the poor.

SOME CHRISTMAS THOUGHTS

CHRISTMAS brings the annual list of good Christmas dinners sent by benevolent rich people to inmates of cottages and union workhouses. The list is accompanied by the annual commentary – how pleasant it is to think that so many poor people have enjoyed a good dinner on Christmas! A more appropriate remark would be – how melancholy to think that it is their only good dinner throughout the year. A good dinner is important only to those with whom it is a rarity. When eating and drinking are the most important feature of festivals, be sure that privation is the rule with the revellers. A bellyful is the *summum bonum* of a savage: he gorges himself to repletion, not knowing when the opportunity may recur. The **unction** with which old chroniclers and village bards dilate on the ale and beef of Christmas-tide, betray a state of society in which a full meal was a god-send. An English Christmas dinner in 1845 differs little from the daily dinner among almost all the comfortable classes. We make believe to feed fatter on Christmas than on any other day of the year because it is the custom – because we think we ought to do so. The sirloins, turkies, candied fruit, and cakes of the season, are insipid to the palates of those who can afford them; they are only enjoyed in imagination by the ragged urchins, the mud-larks, and errand-men, who gather round the shops where they are exposed for sale, wondering, and doubting their senses, which tell them there are so many good things in existence. Yet is Christmas as happy a time, for those to whom Fortune gives to enjoy it, as in the days when a dinner was a dinner indeed. It is a reproach to a society abounding in necessaries and luxuries, like that to which we belong, that there is still a class in it to whom one good dinner in the year is matter for rejoicing. It shows how much has yet to be learned in the economy of social happiness—in the art of distributing the blessings we have earned. We who can earn something owe tithe of our increase to God – that is, to the poor; and we do not clear our scores by sending them lumps of roast-beef and pounds of plum-pudding once a year. It is good that there should be fixed seasons at which an interchange of graceful acts of kindness renews the warmth of affection. Also, eating and drinking are good things in their way. But where the means are so abundant – or might be made so abundant – it is to be desired that they should be kept in their proper place, as subordinate to higher and more spiritual pleasures.

This text is from an article from the *Guardian* newspaper, written in 2013.

Want to volunteer to help homeless people this Christmas? Please don't.

Christmas homeless volunteers are an expensive waste of time for charities. If you want to help, do it for the right reasons

Volunteering to help the homeless at Christmas can be motivated by a combination of sympathy and self-satisfaction.

There's a saying that this time of year brings out the best in people, but fairweather volunteers are the antithesis of this quaint ideal. We've been taking calls from people asking to help out over the Christmas period, all of whom we've turned away.

Cornwall might be a second-home hot spot but for many in the county the hope of having just one home seems out of reach. Homelessness is often considered an urban issue and yet last year's rough sleeper count put Cornwall third in England behind the London boroughs of Westminster and Newham. And those numbers only count the people who are in the system accessing services.

Part of the reason we turn away fairweather volunteers is that the training and vetting programme all our new volunteers have to go through will take longer than the time they're willing to volunteer for. A big part of it, though, is this idea of sympathy rather than empathy. Well-meaning these people may be, but having worked in the sector as long as I have and seen the things I've seen we need to ask the question – who is this desire to volunteer really about?

Many people choose to volunteer at homeless shelters across the country at Christmas time because it makes them feel good to give something back. At our day centre we help 1,000 people a month, our crisis accommodation is full all year round and our 40 two-year temporary accommodation always has a waiting list. Where are these people then? The focus on homelessness at Christmas contributes to its lack of visibility during the rest of the year.

We also, as a society, need to acknowledge the fact that being homeless isn't simply the difference between sleeping outside instead of inside. What is a home? It's a place to feel safe, a measure of empowerment and somewhere people can make positive decisions about their life. It's so much more than a roof, yet public opinion struggles to look beyond the minority of rough sleepers to the millions of people without a permanent home who are stuck in insecure temporary accommodation.

The services we offer to help people are very much shaped by those in need. My own experiences with alcoholism and homelessness helps me in my work, but really it comes from knowing, understanding and listening to our clients. A knowledge you cannot possibly have if you turn up for two weeks a year.

Festive volunteering might seem like a good thing to do but, in most cases, it primarily benefits the volunteer. I believe empathy saves; sympathy harms and it's usually a mixture of sympathy and self-satisfaction that motivates Christmas-only volunteers.

There are no peaks and troughs in the services we offer. We're busy 365 days a year. For those who wish to help us on the other 364 days around Christmas, we'd love to hear from you. But please make it for the right reasons.

Article dated 13 December 2013, by Derek Mace,
Operations manager at Coastline Housing's homelessness service

After you have read each text, compile your ideas about the writers' viewpoints and the language they use in a table like the one below.

Language	Example	Effect or meaning and how this shows viewpoint
Direct statement of feeling or belief	'...how melancholy to think that it is their only good dinner throughout the year'	This follows the self-satisfied 'how pleasant it is to think that so many poor people have enjoyed a good dinner on Christmas!' The writer is building up to criticise the way the rich ease their consciences with a good deed.

 You may have already identified some points of comparison or contrast between the two texts; but, if not, here are some questions to get you started:

- How does the heading of the second text express, fairly directly, the writer's view?

- In the second text, what is the implied meaning of the rhetorical question, 'who is this desire to volunteer really about?' What does the phrase 'fairweather volunteers' suggest?

- How is the article from the *Guardian* about more than just the wish to volunteer? (Look at paragraph 6 and the mention of what 'home' represents.) In what way is this a point of difference or similarity with the *Spectator* article?

- How are the situations or experiences of the two writers different? (Think about what we find out about the writer of the second text, and his own position.)

 Now, consider the methods the writers use to convey their ideas. Look again at the original list of techniques on page 86 and:

- identify if and where any of these have been used

- describe the effect they create in the reader (for example, empathy/sympathy, anger, laughter, shame, reflection, call to act, and so on).

Final task

 Now complete this exam-style task.

For this question, you need to refer to the **whole of the *Spectator* article**, together with **the *Guardian* article**.

Compare how the two writers convey their different views about charitable giving or volunteering at Christmas.

In your answer, you could:

- compare their different views
- compare the methods they use to convey those views
- support your ideas with reference to both texts.

[16 marks]

Checklist for success

✔ Focus closely on specific language choices and analyse what they mean or suggest.

✔ Make sure you compare the perspectives of both writers.

✔ Use connectives to make your points clear and easy to follow (for example, '*While* the writer of Source A says...' or '*Another statement* that demonstrates how strongly...').

Writing to express a viewpoint for Paper 2 Question 5

Assessment objective
- AO5, AO6

How can I express my viewpoint in the most effective ways?

Expressing your viewpoint, whether in articles or letters, or giving a speech about them, requires a range of skills in order to communicate your ideas.

Read this short text:

> The idea of the long school holidays as a parent absolutely appals me. **[1]** Do I really want to spend over five weeks spent trying to occupy the kids? **[2]** It brings to mind interminable car journeys, rainy nights in wet tents and constant searching for public toilets. **[3]** No thanks! **[4]**

1 Identify the features listed below:

   a short minor sentence to emphasise viewpoint

   b trio of three examples supporting viewpoint

   c rhetorical question

   d powerful adverb/verb combination, expressing personal belief

Of course, expressing a point of view requires much more than just one well-structured paragraph. You also need to:

- generate ideas and plan how to structure your points across the whole text

- consider the appropriate tone and **register** for your audience (For example, for a **broadsheet newspaper**, the audience will be educated adults, so the tone will be relatively formal. For a website read by teenagers, the language might be more relaxed and conversational.)

- ensure you express your ideas fluently and accurately. (Remember: 40 per cent of your marks will be for 'technical accuracy' – your spelling, punctuation and grammar.)

Key terms

register: the particular choice of language used, especially in relation to its formality or informality

broadsheet newspaper: newspapers such as *The Times* and the *Daily Telegraph*, which were traditionally set on wider pages so you had to unfold them to read them

Generating ideas and planning your points

You are going to write an article for a broadsheet newspaper in which you argue for or against the following view: 'Christmas and similar festive occasions have become too commercial. It would be better if we didn't celebrate them at all.'

2 To prepare for this task, start by quickly generating ideas around the topic. It may be easier to decide what your view is first.

3 Now, settle on four or five key points (some of your first ideas may not be worth pursuing) and decide which order you will present them in. (Will you put the most important or powerful idea first?)

Structuring your argument

Think about the structure of your paragraphs. Will each one deal just with your own points? Or will you also include the counterarguments and overcome them? For example, note how the student here starts with an argument against his own view, and then responds to it after the connective 'but'.

> *Many shops say customers want the chance to buy in advance, which is why they sell festive goods so early, but I think this just pressurises customers, who feel obliged to start buying.*

If you decide to include counterarguments, you could create an A, B, A2, B2 paragraph structure:

- one paragraph deals with your first point (A)
- the next paragraph states the counterargument (B)
- a new paragraph deals with your next point (A2)
- the next paragraph states the counterargument (B2), and so on.

4 Think of at least two counterarguments to your main points and note them down.

Finally, think about the impact of your sentences. For example:
- short, emphatic sentences work well to hammer home a point
- use longer, more complex sentences to develop more detailed explanations or evidence.

Checklist for success

✔ Consider the tone and register of a broadsheet newspaper. Remember: you do not know your audience; they are mostly educated adults; the paper is a national, not a local, one; the tone should be relatively formal and use Standard English.

✔ Remember layout and structure – use standard paragraphing (you can add an appropriate title to your article if you wish).

Final task

5 Now complete this exam-style task.

'Christmas and similar festive occasions have become too commercial. It would be better if we didn't celebrate them at all.'
Write an article for a broadsheet paper in which you argue for or against this view.

(24 marks for content and organisation
16 marks for technical accuracy)
[40 marks]

End of chapter task

You have seen how the final Stave of *A Christmas Carol* brings the story 'full circle', and this is particularly evident in how Scrooge treats Bob and his family. However, Dickens wants the reader to have some fun with the ending, too.

Read this extract and then answer the question below.

> 'Hallo!' growled Scrooge, in his accustomed voice, as near as he could feign it. 'What do you mean by coming here at this time of day.'
>
> 'I am very sorry, sir,' said Bob. 'I *am* behind my time.'
>
> 'You are?' repeated Scrooge. 'Yes. I think you are. Step this way, sir, if you please.'
>
> 'It's only once a year, sir,' pleaded Bob, appearing from the Tank. 'It shall not be repeated. I was making rather merry yesterday, sir.'
>
> 'Now, I'll tell you what, my friend,' said Scrooge, 'I am not going to stand this sort of thing any longer. And therefore,' he continued, leaping from his stool, and giving Bob such a dig in the waistcoat that he staggered back into the Tank again; 'and therefore I am about to raise your salary!'
>
> Bob trembled, and got a little nearer to the ruler. He had a momentary idea of knocking Scrooge down with it, holding him, and calling to the people in the court for help and a strait-waistcoat.
>
> 'A merry Christmas, Bob!' said Scrooge, with an earnestness that could not be mistaken, as he clapped him on the back. 'A merrier Christmas, Bob, my good fellow, than I have given you for many a year! I'll raise your salary, and endeavour to assist your struggling family, and we will discuss your affairs this very afternoon, over a Christmas bowl of smoking bishop, Bob! Make up the fires, and buy another coal-scuttle before you dot another i, Bob Cratchit.'

1 Starting with this extract, how does Dickens presents Scrooge's conversion in *A Christmas Carol*? Write about how Dickens presents Scrooge's conversion:

- in this extract
- in the novel as a whole.

Check your progress

- I can write clearly about differences in character and ideas within or between texts.
- I can explain clearly what methods a writer uses to convey viewpoint.

- I can show detailed understanding of differences in character and ideas within or between texts
- I can analyse in a detailed way the range of methods a writer uses to convey viewpoint.

The whole text: Plot and character

English Literature

You will re-read:

* Stave One to Stave Five of *A Christmas Carol.*

You will explore:

* how to trace Scrooge's development across the whole of *A Christmas Carol*
* the impact of the other characters on the action and themes of the novel
* how the novel's structure and literary context contribute to its dramatic and thematic purpose.

English Language

You will read:

* an extract from *Black Jack*, a novel by Leon Garfield set in 18th-century London.

You will explore:

* how to evaluate a writer's skills with clear quotations and references to the text.

Evaluating a writer's skills for Paper 1 Question 4

Assessment objective
- AO4

What is evaluation and how can I do it effectively?

When you evaluate a text, you make a judgment about its effectiveness: how well does it achieve its purpose? For example, if you were asked whether you agree with the statement 'Dickens creates a frightening atmosphere in Stave One of *A Christmas Carol* with the appearance of Marley's ghost', you would:

- look for examples of a 'frightening atmosphere' and evidence of the methods Dickens uses to create it
- make some sort of judgment about how these elements made you feel – what *you* found frightening or disturbing.

Of course, in your English Language exam, you will not be faced with a text you know well; you will be asked to evaluate an unfamiliar text. However, the same skills will apply.

Reading and evaluating an unfamiliar text

Read the following extract from *Black Jack*, a novel by Leon Garfield, set in 18th-century London. In it, a young man – Bartholomew Dorking – has been tricked into keeping guard over the body of a hanged murderer, Black Jack, which will be worth money when sold to surgeons. Dorking has been locked in the room until the 'widow' of Black Jack returns.

Black Jack

He banged on the door and shouted 'Help!' five or six times. No one answered: no one came – and his own voice seemed to linger unsuitably in the air. He looked to the coffin, now shrouded in darkness. Had he – had he waked the enormous dead?

Against the faint window he saw Black Jack's feet. They were rooted still in the same patch of air – standing, so to speak, halfway up the window pane…He returned once more to his chair and rested his head against the fireplace wall.

Though he desired strongly to sleep out the hours remaining, sleep would not come. The presence in the coffin seemed to hold it at bay…as if the great death shamed the little one and would not let it come.

Now, little by little, the moon climbed out of the invisible chimney pot, turning the window to dull silver, so that it hung in the dark wall like an old tarnished mirror, capable of nothing but spite.

With a sigh Dorking heard a clock strike nine. His vigil was almost done. He stood up and began to walk softly about the room – to ease the cramp in his legs and ward off the night's chill.

The silver moonlight, very bright now, seemed to lend the dingy room an odd beauty – as if it was intricately fashioned out of shining grey lead. Even the coffin and the still ruffian within it seemed carved and moulded by a master hand.

How finely done was the tangled hair – the knotted brow – the thick, powerful nose…how lifelike were the deep grey lips. How – how miraculously shone the moon in the profound eyes –

In the eyes? In the eyes? Sure to God those eyes had been shut before?

Those eyes! They were open wide! They were moving! They were staring at him!

Bartholomew Dorking, sent from Shoreham to London to be spared the perils of the sea, stood almost dead of terror.

'Alive!' he moaned. 'He's alive!'

More dreadful than violent death itself was this reviving from it.

A deep, rattling sigh filled the room. Black Jack's chest heaved – and his box crackled ominously. His moon-filled eyes rolled fiercely at Bartholomew.

'Alive!' groaned the boy. 'He's alive!'

From *Black Jack* by Leon Garfield (1968)

Developing evaluation skills

At the end of this unit, you will complete an exam-style task on the second half of the *Black Jack* text (from 'Now, little by little…' to the end). In your answer, you need to decide to what extent you agree with this statement:

• 'The writer creates a powerful picture of the transformation from death to life.'

Read through the stages on the next page, to help you prepare your answer to this question.

Stage One: finding examples from the text

 Find references to how the 'dead' man is described, both before he revives and as he comes to life. For example:

- Before: 'carved and moulded by a master hand', 'How finely done was the tangled hair'
- As Jack revives: 'Bartholomew...stood almost dead of terror.'

Aim to add three to four further quotations to the list. Remember, they must be ones that create a 'powerful picture'.

Stage Two: describing your impressions as a reader

 a Now note down your impressions created by these descriptions. For example:

- What do the words 'carved and moulded' make you think of?
- What picture do these words create of the dead man's appearance?
- What image do you get of the boy 'stood almost dead of terror'?

b Write a sentence or two, to explain your impressions. Make sure you use the first person ('I').

You could copy and complete this sentence:

The impression I get from [add suitable example or quotation] *is of...*

Stage Three: explaining your judgment

You can now make a judgment about the writer's use of language, giving reasons for your viewpoint. For example, if you gained a certain impression from a particular quotation, try to say what language devices or methods the author used to achieve this.

 Write two more sentences to describe the effect of the verbs used to describe the 'dead' man. You could start:

The verbs 'carved' and 'moulded' create a powerful image because...	or:	I got a powerful impression of the boy's fear from the phrase 'stood almost dead of terror', as this suggests...

4 Look again at your selected quotations. Decide what is distinctive or effective about the ones you have chosen. For example, you could consider:

- the repetition of particular words or phrases
- the use of punctuation
- the different types of sentences: short, long, questions, exclamations, and so on
- any notable use of imagery (for example, the spooky atmosphere of the room prior to the revival).

Here are two student responses that refer to the 'carved and moulded' quotation:

Student A

> The dead man is described as 'carved and moulded', which is like a sculpture, something you look at and admire. I feel this is a powerful description because these verbs make the vision of the dead man very striking and would be something that would catch your eye.

Student B

> The writer describes the dead man as 'carved and moulded', which means like a statue that has been shaped carefully. These verbs show that something or someone has done this. The boy notices this when the moonlight appears and lights up the face.

5 Which student response *evaluates* the success of the writer better? Why? Give reasons to support your view.

Final task

6 Now complete this exam-style task.

Focus your answer on the section of the passage from 'Now, little by little...' to the end.

A student, having read this section of the text, said: 'The writer creates a powerful picture of the '"transformation from death to life".'

To what extent do you agree?

In your response, you could:

- write about your own impressions of the 'dead' man
- evaluate how the writer has created these impressions
- support your opinions with references to the text.

[20 marks]

Checklist for success

✔ Throughout your answer, any comment or evaluation *must* be linked back to the *core part* of the question: the extent to which the writer is successful in creating a 'powerful picture' of the 'dead' man coming back to life.

✔ Select only four or five quotations relevant to the 'powerful picture' of the transformation.

✔ Include your impressions, using the first person ('I') from time to time.

✔ Say how the writer achieves his effects – describe the language techniques he uses and their impact on the reader.

Analysing Scrooge's development

Assessment objectives
* AO1, AO2, AO3

When and how does Scrooge change as the text progresses?

As part of your exam response, you will have to refer to specific moments in *A Christmas Carol*, but also relate them to the novel as a whole. You will need to be thoughtful and selective about what to include, and effective in dealing with the big picture.

Selecting Scrooge's 'key moments'

It is likely, if you are writing about the way Dickens presents Scrooge, that you will need to refer to one or more of the following aspects:

* Scrooge's initial presentation – how he behaves and speaks at the start of the text
* the young Scrooge – his past lives
* Scrooge's response to what he is shown and how it changes him, and/or his relationship to each of the Spirits, as well as Marley's Ghost
* Scrooge's final transformation and atonement.

1   **a**   First, take a large sheet of paper (for example, A3) and draw a timeline in landscape format for the Staves, as follows:

Stave One ⟶ Stave Two ⟶ Stave Three ⟶ Stave Four ⟶ Stave Five

    b   Under each Stave, write a line of adjectives that best describes Scrooge as he reacts to what he is shown.

    c   Then, under that line, write a second line of adjectives that describes the Scrooge we see in the Spirits' visions of him.

2   Now match each of the following quotations from the text to the timeline (write them in).

1. 'I shall live in the Past, the Present, and the Future!'
2. 'Avarice, hard-dealing, griping cares? They have brought him [the dead man] to a rich end, truly!'
3. '…every idiot who goes about with "Merry Christmas" on his lips should be boiled with his own pudding and buried with a stake of holly through his heart!'
4. 'His face…had begun to wear the signs of care and avarice.'
5. 'a lonely boy was reading near a feeble fire'
6. 'His heart and soul were in the scene, and with his former self.'
7. 'another creature…might have called him father, and been a spring-time in the haggard winter of his life.'

Scrooge's journey

When tracing Scrooge's journey, it is also important to consider *why* he changes. What are the factors that bring about the change?

 3 **a** Read through the list of factors in the table below. For each of these possibilities, decide – on a scale of 1 (not likely) to 10 (very likely) – what the key factors are in Scrooge's transformation.

Factor	1–10
The third Ghost frightens Scrooge and makes him afraid to die	
Scrooge understands more about the state of the poor	
Scrooge sees the results of his acts on society and those around him	
Scrooge sees the specific outcome of his acts and behaviour on himself/what he's become/will be	
Scrooge's soul 'invited' the Spirits in – because deep down he was a good person	
Scrooge is reminded of the happier person he once was	
Scrooge is shown alternative positive visions of Christmas	
Scrooge is loyal to his one friend, Marley, so heeds what he says	
The first two Ghosts influence Scrooge through their questions and statements	

b Provide evidence to back up each of the key factors, as you see them.

4 Scrooge's responses to what he is shown by Marley's Ghost, and then the three Spirits, over the course of *A Christmas Carol*, might be described as an 'emotional rollercoaster'! At various times, Scrooge…

- laughs with joy
- cries and sobs
- shouts
- pleads
- expresses regret
- trembles
- questions
- argues over an issue
- demands answers

When, or at which points, does Scrooge behave like this, and why? Add these to your timeline.

Final task

 5 **a** Complete your own detailed timeline of *A Christmas Carol* that includes:
  - descriptions of Scrooge's state of mind and behaviour (the adjectives and actions)
  - any key quotations (you could include the ones provided here or your own examples).

b When you have completed your timeline, evaluate how the narrative perspective changes during the novel. For example, at what points are we closest to what Scrooge is thinking and feeling?

Analysing the impact of other characters

Assessment objectives
- AO1, AO2

How does Dickens present the other characters and what is their impact on the text?

In your exam, you may be presented with an extract from *A Christmas Carol* that focuses on another character or relationship. In this case, the question is likely to relate to how Dickens uses the character to advance or highlight particular ideas or themes – or how the character is **juxtaposed** with Scrooge.

> **Key term**
>
> **juxtapose:** carefully place ideas or images together to create an effect

1 Read through this list of possible reasons why Dickens may have used different characters in *A Christmas Carol*. Can you identify the characters being referred to?

Shows that kindness as an employer costs little and brings its own rewards	Her appearance suggests that Scrooge had a difficult education and problematic home life	Shows loyalty to Scrooge despite the social and physical consequences of poverty on his family	Demonstrates a belief in Scrooge's possible redemption, and presents a happy and joyful alternative version of Christmas	Shows how her relationship with Scrooge was destroyed by his love of money and how he has suffered for it since

Creating character summaries

2 Now, using the information above and adding any missing elements, complete 'character cards' for each of the secondary characters in *A Christmas Carol*, following the example below.

Character: Fred

Who? Only son of Fan (Scrooge's sister); Scrooge's nephew

Appears: Stave One (visits Scrooge); Stave Three (party); Stave Four (Scrooge's visit)

Characterisation: Presented as a jolly, positive and kind family man

Function: Represents the charitable view that everyone is redeemable; shows Scrooge an alternative version of Christmas that he can access should he change his ways

Relationship with Scrooge and if/how it changes: Cheerful and kind to him but initially unreciprocated. At the end, Scrooge has softened and accepts his friendship.

Key description/quotations: 'I have always thought of Christmas time…as a good time; a kind, forgiving, charitable, pleasant time' (Stave One); 'I am sorry for him [Scrooge]; I couldn't be angry with him if I tried' (Stave Three).

It could be argued that some characters in *A Christmas Carol* are fully rounded, developed characters in their own right, whereas others – who perhaps appear only briefly – are more functional or **symbolic**.

Key term

symbolic: standing for or representing a larger, more important idea or theme

 3
   a Which characters appear just once in the novel?

   b Who appears as a young woman, and then a married mother?

   c Which characters (other than Scrooge) appear at least three times in the text?

   d Are these characters 'fully rounded' or more 'flat' and representational? If the latter, what do they symbolise? Add notes about the depth of their characterisation to your character cards.

Finding out more about Fred

◆ Re-read Stave One, from 'There are many things from which I might have derived good....' to 'I wonder you don't go into Parliament.'

We can explore this section of Stave One in a number of ways in relation to Fred. For example, we can consider:

- what it tells us about Fred *as a character* – and how Dickens *presents him*
- what the *function of the speech is* in relation to the *themes and ideas* in the text
- how Fred's representation is *contrasted with* Scrooge's.

Read one student's comment on one aspect of Fred's speech in this section of Stave One:

> When Fred says about Christmas that 'I believe that it <u>has</u> done me good, and <u>will</u> do me good', the emphatic use of italics suggests his strength of character. It also suggests he has made a conscious effort to think of Christmas in this respect. Fred's words here are juxtaposed with Scrooge's equally forceful words when he reprimands his clerk, showing that strength as Dickens presents it through Fred does not mean being hard or unkind.

 4   Identify those parts of the student's comment that:

- relate to Fred's character
- relate to Fred's function in relation to Scrooge
- relate to wider issues in the novel.

Final task

 5   Now make your own notes on Fred in response to each of the above points. In each case, remember to 'interrogate' what Fred says to infer what we learn about him, as Dickens does not tell us this directly.

Analysing the novel's structure and literary context

Assessment objectives
- AO1, AO2, AO3

How does the novel's structure contribute to its effect?

When we talk about structure in a text, this usually relates to:

- the time or chronology of events – whether things happen in the order they occurred or whether time is disrupted or altered
- the manner in which events are revealed – what we are told as readers, and how these things are introduced or revealed
- patterns and conventions – for example, how chapters open and close, whether events are mirrored or repeated, or how a text conforms with, or contrasts with, other similar texts in the same genre
- forms of narration – who tells the story, and whether the narrator is consistent or changes at points in the text.

The basic structure of A Christmas Carol: the five staves

Each of the staves in *A Christmas Carol* has a specific focus, indicated by its title. However, this only takes us so far. For example, Stave One is called 'Marley's Ghost', but at least half of the Stave is taken up with:

- establishing Scrooge's character through direct description of him, his place of work and later his home
- introducing Fred
- (briefly) mentioning Bob Cratchit, though not by name
- showing Scrooge's interactions with a boy in the street, and the charity collectors.

◆ Re-read Stave One, from the opening up to 'Once upon a time'.

1 How does the time scheme or chronology work in this part of Stave One?

   a What time does this part of the Stave look back to?

   b Why do you think Dickens chose to introduce the phrase 'Once upon a time'? What would this signal to the reader?

2 In order to develop a clear sense of time and events in *A Christmas Carol*, copy and complete a table like the one on the next page. For each Stave:

- add the key scenes or encounters that Scrooge witnesses
- try to add a detail about the time (however general).

> ### Key context
>
> A stave can mean the set of five parallel lines (and the spaces in between) that you see on musical notation or, more commonly, it is an older word meaning the verse of a song.

Stave One	Funeral of Marley – seven years earlier. 'Old' Scrooge introduced Christmas Eve: Fred's visit, charity collectors, carol-singing boy, conversation with clerk/Bob, Scrooge makes his way home, Marley's Ghost
Stave Two	
Stave Three	
Stave Four	
Stave Five	

3 Now trace connections across your table. For example, you could:

- use colour to indicate contrasts in events, or similarities
- circle or underline anything you see as particularly significant.

What links or patterns can you see?

At various times in the text, Scrooge and the Spirits make direct reference to past, present or future events, or recall particular things Scrooge has said or done.

4 Identify:

- who says the following
- the exact context in which it is said in the text
- how it links backwards or forwards. (For example, Marley's chains could link *back* to his own and Scrooge's life as avaricious moneylenders with padlocked safes, or *forward* to Scrooge's 'lightness' in Stave Five.)

'There was a boy singing a Christmas carol at my door last night. I should have liked to have given him something' (Stave Two)

'I wear the chain I forged in life' (Stave One)

'...there he sat alone. Quite alone in the world, I do believe.' (Stave Two)

'God bless us, every one!' said [X] the last of all. (Stave Three)

'Are there no prisons?' said [X]...'Are there no workhouses?' (Stave Three)

Literary contexts: like a fairy story?

Once you read the words 'Once upon a time' in Stave One, it suggests a particular genre of text – the fairy story. But are there really similarities?

Fairy tales often:

- have repeating patterns or encounters (often in trios)
- have a moral message – someone learning something
- involve a quest or journey – the main character overcoming obstacles
- have magical or transformative elements, crossing the realm from reality to fantasy
- have a conflict between good and evil (often represented by characters and/or locations)
- have a happy ending (though not always!).

The highly structured nature of fairy tales is often said to come from the **oral tradition** of stories being told by speakers rather than written down. (In time, of course, the most enduring tales did get recorded in print, and storytellers such as Hans Christian Andersen invented new ones, or adapted older ones.)

Key terms

oral tradition: the passing down of stories through generations by word of mouth

5 Which of the aspects of a fairy tale, listed on page 104, apply to *A Christmas Carol*? Think carefully about each one, then copy and complete a table like the one below. For example, does Scrooge go on a journey? What sort of 'quest' is he on, if any?

Repeating elements	Moral message	Quest or journey	Magic/ transformation	Conflict: good vs evil	Happy ending

6 The main characters of magical fairy stories are often quite down-to-earth – they break through, or defeat, magical elements in order to restore order or good.

   a In what way is Scrooge a 'down-to-earth' character?

   b How does he resist magical elements at various times in the story?

Mythic language

At different points in *A Christmas Carol*, the story veers from a style that is contemporary and immediate to one that sounds almost mythic and timeless.

Re-read these three extracts:

◆ Fan's speech to Scrooge in Stave Two, beginning "Yes!" said the child, brimful of glee' to 'merriest time in all the world'.

◆ The conversation between Belle and Scrooge in Stave Two beginning 'He was not alone...' and ending 'It is enough that I *have* thought of it, and can release you.'

◆ The visit to the ship at sea in Stave Three, starting 'Again the Ghost sped on...' and ending '...they delighted to remember him'.

7 In what ways do each of these three extracts *sound* timeless or like a 'fairy tale'? Make notes on:

• the abstract or representational nature of what is said or done (for example, how does Belle refer to 'Gain' in her conversation with Scrooge?)

• the reference – or lack of it – to everyday, vivid, homely objects or description.

If you are struggling to answer these questions, compare any of these passages with the arrival of the Christmas pudding at the Cratchit table.

Final task

Finally, we can't forget that Dickens subtitled his novel 'A ghost story of Christmas'. This links it, in terms of genre, with other ghost stories that feature visitations from spirits or phantoms. Four of the five Staves in *A Christmas Carol* relate to the appearance of a specific ghost, with a different function on each occasion.

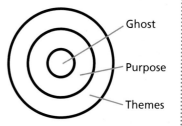

8 For each of the Ghosts in *A Christmas Carol*, create a circle divided into three rings, like the one on the right.

• In the central ring, note the name of the Ghost.

• In the middle ring, note the specific purpose of the Ghost's appearance (as far as Scrooge is concerned).

• In the outer ring, note down any of the themes or motifs to which the Ghost is linked.

End of chapter task

1 For each of the Ghosts in *A Christmas Carol*, write a detailed paragraph based on the model below, explaining:

- the function(s) of the Ghost in the story
- how the Ghost links to the novel's key themes or motifs.

Make sure you include *at least one quotation* that provides evidence of the Ghost's role or purpose.

You can use this writing frame if you wish:

> The [name of Ghost] has several functions.
> First, it…
> Second,…
> It is also important to mention that…

A student has written:

> The function of Marley's Ghost is threefold. First, it frames the main story which is to come, and creates expectations in the reader. Second, it provides information about Scrooge and his former/current life. More importantly, it introduces key themes and motifs, such as the idea that 'mankind' is Scrooge's 'business', not simply trade and money.

Check your progress

- I can explain clearly how Dickens presents characters and structures the plot in *A Christmas Carol*.
- I can use a range of references to support my ideas.

- I can analyse in depth the ways in which Dickens presents characters and structures the plot in *A Christmas Carol*.
- I can use precise, carefully selected references to support my ideas.

The whole text: Themes and contexts

English Literature

You will read:

- Stave One to Stave Five of *A Christmas Carol*.

You will explore:

- some of the settings in the novel and what they reveal about wider themes and contexts
- the different perspectives on the poor that Dickens presents in *A Christmas Carol*
- how Dickens uses the supernatural as a dramatic device
- why the section about Ignorance and Want in Stave Three is so important.

Exploring themes through key settings

Assessment objectives
• AO2, AO3

How can I link my knowledge of the settings in *A Christmas Carol* to social context and themes?

Dickens is very specific about the locations he uses, whether in the city or beyond it.

Where setting is a key aspect of any passage you are given in the exam, it is important that you can comment on the setting's function in the novel and how it links to social context and themes.

Dickens's choice of settings in *A Christmas Carol*

Dickens chooses particular settings in *A Christmas Carol* for a range of reasons, such as:

- to show that the Christmas spirit is alive and well, even in the most unlikely places
- to explore the past and its effect on the present and future
- to reflect the character of the person or people associated with the place
- to mirror the mood or tone of the moment.

1 For each of the four settings below from *A Christmas Carol*:

   a identify the setting
   b locate it in the novel
   c read the rest of the description of the setting (where you found it in the novel).

1. 'a gloomy suite of rooms, in a lowering pile of building up a yard' (Stave One)

2. 'a mansion of dull red brick…a large house, but one of broken fortunes' (Stave Two)

3. 'a dismal reef of sunken rocks, some league or so from shore' (Stave Three)

4. 'overrun by grass and weeds, the growth of vegetation's death, not life; choked up with too much burying' (Stave Four)

2 Now consider the four reasons Dickens chooses particular settings.

Copy and complete a table like the one below. For each setting, add any links to social context and wider themes.

Setting	Reasons Dickens chose it	Links to social context and wider themes

Linking setting to themes and contexts

Now look again at how Dickens describes one setting, in this passage from Stave Three:

> The sky was gloomy, and the shortest streets were choked up with a dingy mist, half thawed, half frozen, whose heavier particles descended in a shower of sooty atoms…There was nothing very cheerful in the climate or the town, and yet there was an air of cheerfulness abroad that the clearest summer air and brightest summer sun might have endeavoured to diffuse in vain.
>   For the people who were shovelling away on the house-tops were full of glee…

3 Start by selecting some key quotations from the passage. For example, make notes in response to the following questions.
  • How does Dickens describe the sky, the streets and the mist?
  • How does Dickens describe the mood among the citizens, despite this?

A student has started to write a paragraph linking the description to the context:

> The 'shower of sooty atoms' which fall from the sky in this description is a reminder of the very real health concerns people faced during rapid industrialisation in Victorian times. However, the important theme Dickens explores here is not the impact of industry on living conditions, but…

4 What link to context has been made here?

5 Now copy and complete the paragraph above, adding a comment about the theme of Christmas and how it affects people. Try to include a relevant quotation to support your point.

Final task

6 Choose from one of the four settings described under Question 1.
Write two paragraphs about your chosen setting.
In the first paragraph, explain:
  • what mood or atmosphere the description creates
  • how the description of the setting links to wider themes and/or social contexts.
In the second paragraph, explain:
  • how the description links with or contrasts with other settings in the novel.

Analysing themes: perspectives on poverty

Assessment objectives
- AO2, AO3

How does Dickens present the poor in *A Christmas Carol*?

In *A Christmas Carol,* Dickens presents the poor in a variety of situations. It is important to consider how these situations vary, while at the same time developing a sense of how Dickens views the poor overall.

How Dickens presents the needs of the poor

Re-read the following sections of *A Christmas Carol*, which relate especially to general ideas about society and the poor. Make brief notes in response to the questions that follow.

1 Read Stave One, the visit of the charity collectors, from 'At this festive time of year...' to 'It's not my business'.

    a What do the charity collectors say 'Many thousands' and 'hundreds of thousands' lack?

    b What is Scrooge's response to the needs of the poor as explained by the charity collectors?

    c What impression do we get from the charity collectors of the institutions Scrooge mentions?

    d What is Scrooge's response to the idea that many of the poor 'would rather die'?

2 Read Stave One, from 'Oh! captive bound...' to '...which its light would have conducted *me*!'

    a What does Marley say should have been his 'business'?

    b What powerful metaphor does Marley use to compare the relative importance of his 'trade' with what should have been his real 'business'?

3 Read Stave Two, from 'Another idol has displaced me...' to 'such severity as the pursuit of wealth!'

In Stave Two, poverty – or fear of it – becomes a point of conflict between Scrooge and Belle.

    a In the Bible, idolatry was the worship of something other than God. What does Belle say Scrooge worships?

    b What does Scrooge give as his reason for worshipping this thing?

Interpreting Scrooge's motives

4 Overall, how would you sum up Scrooge's attitude by the end of his conversation with Belle (taking into account what he says and how he is presented in Stave One)?

Look at each of the interpretations below and decide which, if any, are closest to your reading of Scrooge's attitude.

Interpretation 1: Poverty brings hardship; Scrooge believes it is best to look after yourself by earning as much as you can, and keeping it.

Interpretation 2: Scrooge feels the state provides for the poor – so what has poverty got to do with him?

Interpretation 3: Scrooge would like to help, but poverty doesn't affect him, so why should he worry?

Interpretation 4: Scrooge despises the poor, or those who waste money unnecessarily. He thinks they are weak and deserve what they get.

For each interpretation you agree with, make sure you can back up your views with reference to what Scrooge says or does in the first two Staves.

Different perspectives on poverty

Scrooge's is not the only perspective on poverty. Dickens, as narrator, presents some alternatives.

	Descriptions of poverty
Stave Three	• The lengths the Cratchits go to make ends meet (consider the Christmas meal, their clothing, references to work) • Tiny Tim's appearance and physical condition • The faces of Ignorance and Want at the end of the Stave (consider the particular adjectives to describe them)
Stave Four	• Old Joe's place, his companions and the part of London where they live

5 For each of these descriptions of poverty in the table above:

a Find at least two quotations that show the *effect* of poverty on either appearance or behaviour.

b Decide which perspective below is represented by each description.

Dickens's perspectives on poverty
Poverty as a corrupting, immoral influence
Poverty as degrading and shameful
Poverty as revealing people's decency and pride
Poverty as as a direct result of poor education

Final task

6 Poverty is shown to have a range of effects in *A Christmas Carol*. Write 100 words explaining:
- what the worst effects of poverty are in the novel
- what the 'good' effects of poverty are, if any.

Make sure you select at least one relevant quotation for the worst effects, and one for the 'good' effects as well.

Analysing the function of the supernatural

Assessment objectives
- AO2, AO3

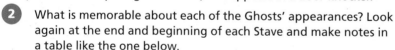

How does Dickens use the supernatural in *A Christmas Carol*?

You have already explored the main function of the Ghosts in *A Christmas Carol* (to reform Scrooge). However, the Ghosts are not simply plot devices; they also add significantly to mood, and link with wider themes and ideas.

The supernatural as dramatic device

The Ghosts in *A Christmas Carol* make an exciting and memorable impression on the reader.

1 Which Ghost is being referred to in each of these descriptions?

- 'Its hair, which hung about its neck and down its back, was white as if with age; and yet the face had not a wrinkle in it'
- 'Its dark brown curls were long and free; free as its genial face, its sparkling eye, its open hand'
- '...behind the dusky shroud, there were ghostly eyes intently fixed up on him [Scrooge]'
- 'the spirit raised a frightful cry, and shook its chain with such a dismal and appalling noise'

Part of the Ghosts' impact is that they are so different – such that we, as readers, do not know what to expect from them. Expectations are also confounded by *how* each one appears; even Marley's Ghost, which is perhaps the least surprising of the four, first appears in a door-knocker.

2 What is memorable about each of the Ghosts' appearances? Look again at the end and beginning of each Stave and make notes in a table like the one below.

Ghost	How and where it appears	Key description	Overall effect
Marley's Ghost			
Ghost of Christmas Past	Appears at Scrooge's bedside – 'found himself face to face with the unearthly visitor'		The ghost is almost like a reflection of Scrooge himself – an old man and a boy at the same time
Ghost of Christmas Present		'a jolly Giant, glorious to see'	
Ghost of Christmas Yet to Come	Appears across the ground 'like a mist' towards Scrooge, directly after the other Spirit disappears		

Read this account of Marley's Ghost, which is taken from a student essay on the use of the supernatural in *A Christmas Carol*.

> Marley's Ghost perhaps conforms to our expectations of ghosts with its 'heavy chain', and we enjoy the gruesome moment when its 'jaw dropped down'. However, it is also important that it is still recognisably Marley – a real person – so that Scrooge is able to make the connection between his life now and what awaits him if he continues to live as he does.

— explains our response as readers to the Ghost

— begins to explain the function of the Ghost

3 Is the final sentence entirely correct? If Marley's Ghost creates such an impact, why are the Three Spirits needed?

Add a sentence to the student's paragraph above, to explain Scrooge's lack of understanding at this point in the novel.

How Dickens 'uses' the supernatural

Consider the diagram below, which summarises the different ways in which Dickens uses the supernatural in *A Christmas Carol.*

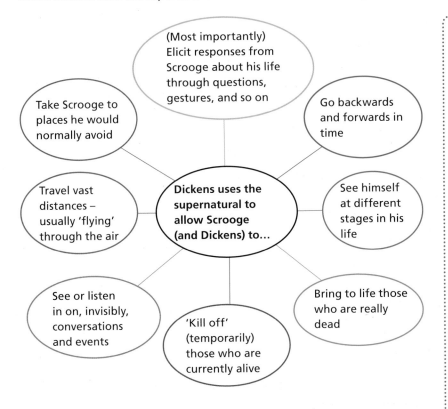

Final task

5 In *A Christmas Carol*, which of the four Ghosts makes the greatest impact on you as reader? Write at least two paragraphs explaining your thoughts. Remember to:

- explain what the Ghost is like, how it appears and its effect on Scrooge
- discuss the Ghost's function(s) (use the diagram to the left) and impact on the story as a whole
- quote carefully to support your ideas.

4 For each of the above points, find and note down an example from the novel.

Revising a key idea: Ignorance and Want

Assessment objectives
- AO2, AO3

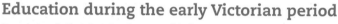

Why is the section about Ignorance and Want in Stave Three so important?

In Lesson 4.4 (pages 54–55), we explored the section in Stave Three when the Ghost of Christmas Present reveals the two children Ignorance and Want. Their appearance provides a focal point in *A Christmas Carol*. So why are these two figures so important to the novel?

You may recall that, at the start of his writing career, Dickens observed the poor in his walks around London, and that many of his observations found their way into *Sketches by Boz* (for example, see Lesson 5.1, page 60). You have also read about infant mortality during the Victorian period (see Lesson 5.2, page 62) and Dickens's own anger at working conditions in factories (see Lesson 1.2, pages 14–15).

So what about education? In Lesson 3.4 (pages 38–43) you looked at Dickens's Ragged School letter, but what was the national education system like during his lifetime?

Education during the early Victorian period

Read the following background information and the extract below.

A number of reports [in the early Victorian period] highlighted the deficiencies and called for more and better schools. One such report looked at 12,000 parishes in 1816, and found that 3,500 had no school, 3,000 had **endowed schools** of varying quality, and 5,500 had **unendowed schools** of even more variable quality.

From *Education in England: A Brief History*, by Derek Gillard (2011)

Key context

By 1835, 1.45 million out of 1.75 million children went to school; however, the average time they spent there was just one year. By 1851, the average time children remained in education had risen to two years, but among the very poorest this figure would have been considerably less.

Glossary

endowed school: a school given money through permanent trusts or grants to educate either poor or middle-class children

unendowed school: a school that relied on charity or donations

An article about 'pauper children'

Now read this extract from an article that Dickens wrote in 1850, about pauper children who were sent to Norwood School. Dickens wrote the letter several years after writing *A Christmas Carol* (published 1843), but many of his concerns in the letter mirror the concerns he expressed in the novel.

> They are the very dregs of the population of the largest city in the world – the human waifs and strays of the modern **Babylon**; the children of poverty, and misery, and crime; in very many cases labouring under physical defects, such as bad sight or hearing; almost always stunted in their growth, and bearing the stamp of ugliness and suffering on their features. Generally born in dark alleys and back courts, their playground has been the streets, where the wits of many have been prematurely sharpened at the expense of any morals they might have.
>
> From *Household Words 1* (1850), No.23, pages 549–552

Glossary

Babylon: an ancient city reputed to be the largest in the world, but also morally corrupt and on the path to ruin

1 What 'defects' does Dickens say these uneducated children have?

2 What does Dickens say the effect of having the streets as a 'playground' has had on the children?

Exploring the context

◆ Re-read Stave Three, from 'Forgive me if I am not justified in what I ask...' to 'The bell struck twelve.'

3 How are the effects of Want or Ignorance indicated by the description of the children? Make notes about:
- their physical appearance and behaviour
- the effect these descriptions might have had on a reader in Dickens's day.

4 In what ways does this description of the children Want and Ignorance mirror the descriptions of the real pauper children Dickens observed at Norwood?

Final task

5 Why is the section about Ignorance and Want in Stave Three so important? Write your own explanation commenting on the issues of the time and how these influenced Dickens's writing in *A Christmas Carol*.

End of chapter task

Look at this cartoon from *Punch* magazine, dated 3 July 1858. It was intended as a complaint about the illness and disease caused by how dirty the River Thames was.

PUNCH, OR THE LONDON CHARIVARI.—JULY 3, 1858.

FATHER THAMES INTRODUCING HIS OFFSPRING TO THE FAIR CITY OF LONDON.

(A Design for a Fresco in the New Houses of Parliament.)

DIPHTHERIA.　SCROFULA.　CHOLERA.

 1　Explore the context related to the image by making notes under these headings:

- Who was the cartoon meant for (according to the caption)? (Note: a 'fresco' is a wall painting.)
- How is the cartoonist using a similar technique to the one Dickens used in Stave Three with the appearance of Want and Ignorance?
- Search online for images of Want and Ignorance as artists have depicted them. Can you find one that best represents the way Dickens describes them?

Check your progress

- I can explain clearly how Dickens presents ideas, themes and contexts in *A Christmas Carol*.
- I can use a range of references to support my ideas.

- I can analyse in depth the ways in which Dickens presents ideas, themes and contexts in *A Christmas Carol*.
- I can use precise, carefully selected references to support my ideas.

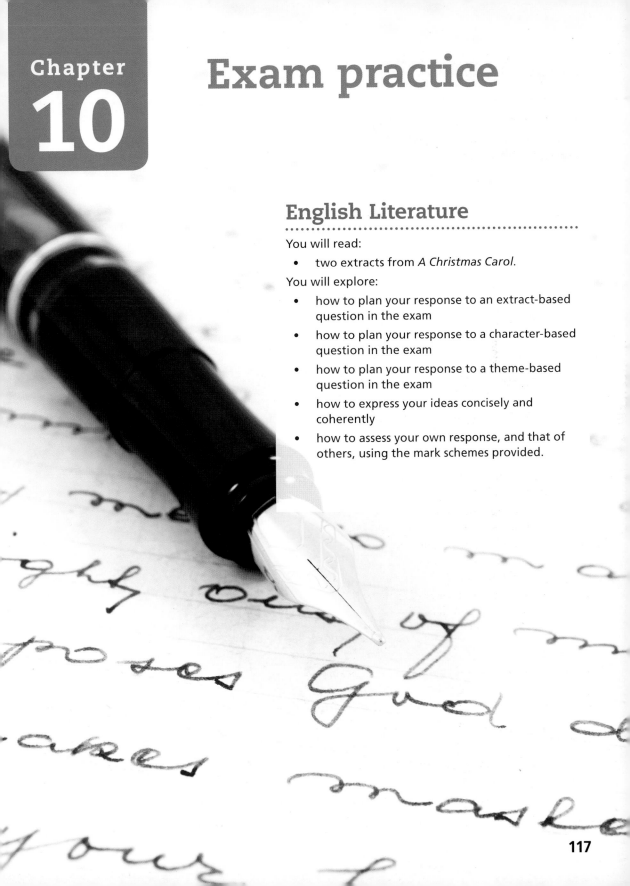

Chapter 10

Exam practice

English Literature

You will read:

- two extracts from *A Christmas Carol*.

You will explore:

- how to plan your response to an extract-based question in the exam
- how to plan your response to a character-based question in the exam
- how to plan your response to a theme-based question in the exam
- how to express your ideas concisely and coherently
- how to assess your own response, and that of others, using the mark schemes provided.

Understanding the task

Assessment objectives
• AO1, AO2, AO3

How should I respond to an extract-based question on character in the exam?

In this section, you will read an extract from *A Christmas Carol* and plan your answer to a character-based exam-style question.

1 Read the following extract and the task that follows it.

Read the following extract from Stave Three and then answer the question that follows.

In this extract, Scrooge has been observing the Cratchit household and is questioning the Ghost of Christmas Present.

'Spirit,' said Scrooge, with an interest he had never felt before, 'tell me if Tiny Tim will live.'

'I see a vacant seat,' replied the Ghost, 'in the poor chimney-corner, and a crutch without an owner, carefully preserved. If these shadows remain unaltered by the Future,
5   the child will die.'

'No, no,' said Scrooge. 'Oh, no, kind Spirit! say he will be spared.'

'If these shadows remain unaltered by the Future, none other of my race,' returned the Ghost, 'will find him here. What then? If he be like to die, he had better do it, and decrease the surplus population.'
10   Scrooge hung his head to hear his own words quoted by the Spirit, and was overcome with penitence and grief.

'Man,' said the Ghost, 'if man you be in heart, not adamant, forbear that wicked cant until you have discovered What the surplus is, and Where it is. Will you decide what men shall live, what men shall die? It may be, that in the sight of Heaven, you are more
15   worthless and less fit to live than millions like this poor man's child. Oh God! to hear the Insect on the leaf pronouncing on the too much life among his hungry brothers in the dust!'

Scrooge bent before the Ghost's rebuke, and trembling cast his eyes upon the ground.

---

0 1 Starting with this extract, how does Dickens present Scrooge as a transformed member of society?

Write about:

• how Dickens presents Scrooge in this extract

• how Dickens presents Scrooge as transformed in the novel as a whole. **[30 marks]**

2   Begin by **highlighting the key elements** in the question you need to address. For example:

Key element in question	AO covered	What you need to do
Scrooge...transformed	AO1 – your understanding and response	This is a *character* question; so you must focus on the author's presentation of **Scrooge** as someone who changes (and not anyone else) with appropriate evidence.
How does **Dickens present**...	AO2 – what the writer does	Focus on *what Dickens does* – his language and structural choices.
member of society	AO3 – the social context	This part of the question links to *context*, so make sure you include relevant comment on the social context as it is presented in the passage and the novel (not just what you know of Victorian society).

3   You now need to deal with part of **AO1 – gathering evidence**.

   a   Start with the **extract** first. **Jot down two or three ideas** about how it shows Scrooge as 'transformed'. For this, you need to find:

- specific references to Scrooge
- any **relevant quotations** that tell the reader *how* Scrooge has changed.

   b   Now think about Scrooge **in the rest of the novel**. As this is about 'transformation', you probably need to note down how Dickens presented Scrooge originally. Note down **one or two quotations or examples** of what Scrooge was like *before* the arrival of the ghosts.

4   Now, consider **AO2 – what Dickens does as a writer**. For example, consider how Dickens uses:

- **structural effects** – for example, how events show Scrooge's former and changed self in the extract and earlier in the text
- **language effects** – for example, starting with the extract, how Scrooge's short emphatic 'No, no' shows his desperation, or how the verb 'trembling' compares with the 'hard and sharp as flint' depiction in Stave One
- more **general characterisation** – for example, other aspects of Scrooge's speech, movements and interactions with others.

5   Finally, consider **AO3 – the social context**. Jot down any points that arise from the extract. For example:

- Why does Scrooge ask about Tiny Tim? How does this link with Dickens's views about social responsibility?
- Why does the Ghost talk about the 'surplus population', and how does this link with Scrooge's earlier words? How is this linked to Dickens's own views about poverty and how it should be tackled?

6   Once you have your notes, decide on a plan. Write down your **five or six main points**. The order of your essay is up to you.

Developing your response

Assessment objective
• AO1

> How can I do justice to my ideas through the way I write?

Your opening paragraph

There are a number of ways you can begin your essay in the exam, but the main thing to remember is to make a clear point in response to the essay focus. For example, you could:

A. Re-state **what is happening in the extract** in particular reference to **the idea of Scrooge being transformed**. This could be a comment on the significance of the extract moment in the wider context of the novel. For example:

> In this extract, we see Scrooge…This extract is particularly relevant to his transformation as…

B. Make a **wider comment** or statement about Scrooge's transformation **in the novel as a whole**. This could be a comment on what sort of transformation occurs, and whether it is a private or social change. For example:

> In the novel, Dickens presents a man who…The change he undergoes is one where…

If you choose Approach A, you may not want to 'use up' one of your key quotations – but to save it for the main body of the essay. If you choose Approach B, a quotation that sums up Scrooge's change would be useful; for example, Scrooge saying 'I am not the man I was' in Stave Four.

If you would like to begin your essay in a different way, that is fine too!

1   Draft your opening paragraph.

Writing effective paragraphs in the main body of the response

At a basic level, **each paragraph** about the passage should:

- **make a relevant point** about how Dickens presents Scrooge (as transformed or otherwise)
- **support that point** with direct reference to the text – preferably a succinct (not too long) quotation
- **explain or further explore the point**
- if possible, **link with or compare/contrast with a point about Scrooge elsewhere** in the novel or within the same extract (if you wish to leave wider comments for later).

For comments about **the text as a whole**, you could concisely refer to key events or actions without quotations, provided it is clear what and who you are referring to – and at what point in the text.

Remember: this is a guide to ordering your paragraphs only. To bring interest to your writing, try to vary the order of your paragraphs – for example, you could begin with a quotation or by explaining an idea.

Here is one student's paragraph in response to the task above:

In the extract, Dickens provides an example of Scrooge's earlier views when the Ghost questions him. The Ghost compares him to 'the insect on the leaf' who wishes to decide his fellow creatures' fate. Dickens is asking whether such an insignificant being has the right to take away life. Dickens's description of Scrooge's response, using the verb 'trembling', as if he is a sinner in church, shows him transformed from Stave One, when he 'walked out with a growl'.

2 In the student's paragraph above, identify:
   a   the **topic sentence** that introduces the main point
   b   the **embedded quotations** taken from the extract
   c   the basic explanation of the quotation
   d   the exploration that tells us more
   e   the link to another part of the novel.

3 Consider your final paragraph.

   It:
   • should briefly sum up your overall argument, but do so concisely and without listing previous points
   • should present a distilled version of what you have explored
   • may even use a further relevant quotation. For example, here is one student's ending:

As the extract shows, Dickens presents Scrooge as someone who has been utterly exposed by the experiences he has had, so that at this moment he begins to cast off the layers of avarice and self-interest. It is already clear in the extract that he is 'not the man' he once was.

4 Now write your response in full paragraphs to the exam-style question, based on the plan you created in Lesson 10.1 (pages 118–119).

Key term

topic sentence: sentence that tells the reader what the main, or overall, focus of a paragraph is

embedded quotation: short quotation inserted fluently into the sentence

Peer- and self-assessment

Assessment objectives
• AO1, AO2, AO3

Before you make an evaluation of how well you have answered the exam-style question, check the advice below. It will help you decide whether your work falls broadly into the first or the second category – or outside them.

What do the AOs actually mean?

AO1	• **AO1** is about your *understanding* of the task, and how you respond to it – the expression of your ideas, your use of quotations and evidence from the text.
AO2	• **AO2** is about you *showing what you know about the writer's choices and the effects* they have on the reader: for example, vocabulary and language devices (such as imagery), and use of structure or form (order of events, how things happen, language patterns or sequences).
AO3	• **AO3** is about *showing you understand particular views or background information related to context* and how these link to the task set. For example, this could be ideas the writer has about society that arise from the text, settings or other details.

What are the features of a graded response at different levels?

	Features of a clear and well-explained response (Grade 5)	Features of a convincing, analytical response (Grade 7+)
AO1	• You show you have **understood the task clearly**, so your points are **relevant**. You comment on **both the passage and the wider novel**. • You make **clear and suitable references** to the text (that support your points effectively) and your **use of quotations is clearly explained**. It is likely you have embedded most or all of the quotations in your writing.	• You have a **complete, deep understanding of the task** and put forward a **sustained response**. You take in the **bigger picture** and are able to **connect your ideas** into a **coherent overall view** of the task and text. • Any references you make to the text are **extremely carefully selected** and are more fruitful than alternatives you might have chosen. You show exploration and more than one **interpretation** of a **wide range of language, form** and **structural aspects**.
AO2	• You **explain the writer's methods** clearly so that the marker knows what particular things the author has done. • You **explain clearly what the effects of the writer's choices are**. • You use some **useful subject terminology** (for example, reference to 'adjectives' or 'irony') in a correct way, supporting the points you make.	• You **analyse the writer's methods**, drilling down into detail where needed, or expanding interpretations to make **interesting and useful links**. • You use a **wide range of subject terminology**, and explore **in detail** the **potential and varying effects** on the reader.

	Features of a clear and well-explained response (Grade 5)	Features of a convincing, analytical response (Grade 7+)
AO3	• You **show clear understanding** of how some ideas about **context link** to the **set task.** • You do not 'bolt on' irrelevant references about social or historical ideas, or about the writer's views, but **make a straightforward** link to the task.	• Your comments on context are **convincing and significantly add to your analysis** of the text. • You reveal **rich insights** into writer's motives and the overall 'message' of the text, all linked convincingly to the task set.

1 Go through your own response to the exam-style question on page 118. If possible, write your own brief annotations around it. Ideally, these should be linked to the Assessment Objectives. For example, consider how this has been done below for the student's paragraph from Lesson 10.2 (page 121).

AO1 – shows a clear understanding of this part of the text

In this extract, Dickens provides an example of Scrooge's earlier views when the Ghost questions him. The Ghost compares him to 'the insect on the leaf' who wishes to decide his fellow creatures' fate. Dickens is asking whether such an insignificant being has the right to take away life. Dickens's description of Scrooge's response, using the verb 'trembling', as if he is a sinner in church, shows him transformed from Stave One, when he 'walked out with a growl'.

AO1 and AO2 – selects a relevant quotation and explains what the quotation means

AO1 and AO3 – further explanation of a more complex meaning, touching on wider ideas about social responsibility and action

AO2 reference to the verb helps develop the point made

Apply what you have learned

Look again at your own work and follow this process:
✔ Read the two sample answers by Student A and Student B and the examiner's comments on them (pages 124–127).
✔ Look again at the AO marking criteria for the Grade 5 and Grade 7+ responses (in the above table).
✔ Evaluate your own response and the level you think it is closest to.
✔ Then, find a paragraph in your work that you think requires improvement or development.
✔ Identify which aspects from the AOs you need to improve in your chosen paragraph.
✔ Re-draft or rewrite the paragraph, applying the changes you think are needed.

2 Now read the following sample response to the exam-style question on page 118 and the examiner's comments and overview.

Student A

In this extract, Scrooge has been shown Christmas at the Cratchits and how they manage to enjoy it, even though they are quite poor. Scrooge has learned about Tiny Tim and this has had an effect on him. You could say this is when he gets it for the first time – what happens if you don't act to help the poor.

> **AO1** – clear understanding of how the passage fits in the novel

> **AO1 and AO2** – attempt at interpreting Scrooge's behaviour, but expression is a bit informal

Scrooge is clearly affected by what he sees. Dickens says he speaks 'with an interest he never felt before'. It is like the first time reality has made him feel sympathy for anyone. He begs the Spirit to make sure Tiny Tim is safe, but the Ghost makes it clear that change needs to happen – 'If these shadows remain unaltered by the Future...' – or Tim will die.

> **AO1** – appropriate quotation to support the point

Dickens shows that Scrooge is transformed when he says he 'hung his head' when the Ghost reminds him of what he said earlier. This was a reference to the Malthusian idea that population growth caused poverty. Scrooge referred to this when he dismissed the charity collectors in Stave One, but Dickens shows that Scrooge hadn't really thought it through. The two nouns 'penitence' and 'grief' explain how he feels now.

> **AO2** – clear reference to effect of language used about Scrooge

> **AO3** – simple reference to political idea of the time, though not developed

Also, Dickens shows Scrooge's change through his physical movements: it says he 'bent' and 'trembling cast his eyes upon the ground'. These actions show his feelings of guilt and shame, very different from the 'Humbug!' of Stave One.

> **AO1 and AO2** – attempt to widen focus to the rest of the novel, but quotation not fully explained

Dickens shows Scrooge's real change much later, though. In the early part of the book he shows that Scrooge responds with emotion to what he sees, for example, when he comments in Stave Two on how Fezziwig made people happy without spending much money, but he hasn't really changed at this point.

> **AO1** – clear point about Scrooge and change, linked to other parts of the novel

The real transformation only comes at the end of Stave Four when he realises he is the dead man who no one loves. In the graveyard, he tells the last Ghost – 'I will not shut out the lessons that they teach.' He means the different Christmases he has seen and suggests he will open his heart to change and act upon it.

Overall, the passage gives hints of him changing and then the process has a bigger impact, especially when he sees the future. Then in the final Stave, Dickens shows him helping society by promising to make a big donation to charity and being a 'second father' to Tiny Tim. Many Victorians believed that it was your responsibility to help yourself but Dickens shows that you don't have to be like that. Like Scrooge, you can change and help society when the poor can't help themselves.

AO1 – clearly expressed topic sentence introduces another section of the novel

AO3 – a general point about social responsibility and its link to Scrooge's transformation

Examiner's comment

This is a clear, well-argued response that addresses both the passage and the novel. Quotations and textual references are almost always well chosen and relevant. On occasions, greater analysis of individual words and phrases, and more detailed exploration of contextual links, would have added greater depth and insight. There is also the odd informal turn of phrase.

3 Evaluate this answer and decide which of the two levels (Grade 5 or 7+) from the AO marking criteria table on pages 122–123 it is closer to.

4 Now read the next sample response to the exam-style question on page 118 and the examiner's comments.

Student B

Over the novel as a whole, Dickens shows us a man who is transformed by his experiences. From the hard-hearted miser at the start, 'solitary as an oyster', Scrooge is later presented as 'as good a man, as the good old city knew'. The main thing to note is that Scrooge's change isn't just personal, for his own sake or his family's, but for the 'city' – he is helping society.

AO1 – opening sentence sets up overall picture of novel

AO1 – interprets Scrooge's 'journey', focusing clearly on him as a 'member of society'

The passage is not where Scrooge's transformation starts: Dickens has already shown the reader Scrooge's response to himself as a carefree young apprentice at Fezziwig's, and later in the same Stave when we see how he lost Belle through his love of money. However, the passage is important because it shows him beginning to understand the effects of his unkindness on society as a whole.

AO1 – answer sustains focus on Scrooge's response to society in relation to the passage

For example, when Dickens describes Scrooge asking if Tim will live 'with an interest he had never felt before', the phrase 'never felt before' shows that he is emotionally ready to be less selfish. Yet at this time Scrooge doesn't realise it is up to him to change. When he pleads with the Ghost saying, 'say he will be spared, he thinks that just by caring about Tiny Tim that is enough. In a way this could be a criticism of Victorian churchgoers, who prayed and thought they were virtuous but didn't actually do anything practical to help the poor.

AO2 – analyses effect of selected quotation

AO3 – explores contextual idea and Dickens's response to it

Dickens also uses a form of structural juxtaposition in this passage, when the Ghost reminds Scrooge of his own words from Stave One, when he told the charity collectors that the poor 'would rather die' and 'decrease the surplus population'. This Malthusian concept had been attractive to Scrooge as a theoretical idea, but he now sees what it means in practice – there will be a 'vacant seat'. This is why he is 'overcome with penitence and grief'. These two abstract nouns are important. By regretting what he has done, he has taken the first step towards rectifying things.

AO1 and AO2 – well-expressed comment on Dickens'd use of structure across the novel

AO3 – contextual reference used to explore Scrooge's development

AO2 – detailed focus on Dickens's language choices

'Grief' shows he feels for Tiny Tim as though he had actually died. Nevertheless, it will take until Stave Five for Scrooge to rectify his earlier actions, which is where Dickens's structural balancing of Scrooge's old and new selves comes full circle.

Dickens provides a picture of Scrooge's misguided views when the Ghost questions him. The Ghost's analogy compares him to 'the insect on the leaf' who wishes to decide his fellow creatures' fate. Dickens seems to be asking whether such an insignificant being has the right to take away life. Dickens's description of Scrooge's response, using the verb 'trembling' as if he is a sinner in church, shows him transformed from Stave One, when he 'walked out with a growl'.

AO2 – further reference to Dickens's use of language device

The specific changes for Scrooge as a 'member of society' mainly come in the final Stave. While making Scrooge claim at the end of Stave Four that he is 'not the man I was', Dickens goes on to show Scrooge's promises put into practice. So, Dickens's use of the adverb to show how he behaves with people as he passes them on the street – 'irresistibly pleasant' – suggests there is a great wave of happiness in him that can't be held back.

AO1 – shows understanding of wider structural elements

Scrooge's promises in the final Stave to contribute even more money to charity show that he is transformed into a responsible member of society. This is perhaps a message from Dickens to his readers that whatever their circumstances they all have responsibilities for the greater good, and that Christianity meant behaving like a Christian not just thinking like one. This is emphasised by the fact that Scrooge raises Bob's wages, and becomes a 'second father' to Tiny Tim, indicating how far he will go to transform his old life of avarice and solitude.

AO3 – detailed interpretation of contextual idea linked to task

Examiner's comment

This is a convincingly argued response that moves seamlessly between an overview of the novel and specific exploration of the passage. References to social context are used to support the overall argument and Dickens's use of language and structure is explored in depth, with evidence of personal interpretation.

5 Evaluate this answer and decide which of the two levels (Grade 5 or 7+) from the AO marking criteria table on pages 122–123 it is closer to.

In what ways is Student B's answer a more effective response than Student A's?

Understanding the task

Assessment objectives
• AO1, AO2, AO3

How should I respond to an extract-based question on a theme in the exam?

In this section, you will read an extract from *A Christmas Carol* and plan your answer to a theme-based exam-style question.

1 Read the following extract and the task that follows it.

Read the following extract from Stave One and then answer the question that follows.

In this extract, Marley's Ghost has appeared to Scrooge and is speaking to him.

> 'Oh! captive, bound, and double-ironed,' cried the phantom, 'not to know, that ages of incessant labour, by immortal creatures, for this earth must pass into eternity before the good of which it is susceptible is all developed. Not to know that any Christian spirit working kindly in its little sphere, whatever it may be, will find its mortal life too short
>
> 5 for its vast means of usefulness. Not to know that no space of regret can make amends for one life's opportunity misused! Yet such was I! Oh! such was I!'
>
> 'But you were always a good man of business, Jacob,' faltered Scrooge, who now began to apply this to himself.
>
> 'Business!' cried the Ghost, wringing its hands again. 'Mankind was my business. The
> 10 common welfare was my business; charity, mercy, forbearance, and benevolence, were, all, my business. The dealings of my trade were but a drop of water in the comprehensive ocean of my business!'
>
> It held up its chain at arm's length, as if that were the cause of all its unavailing grief, and flung it heavily upon the ground again.
>
> 15 'At this time of the rolling year,' the spectre said, 'I suffer most. Why did I walk through crowds of fellow beings with my eyes turned down, and never raise them to that blessed Star which led the Wise Men to a poor abode! Were there no poor homes to which its light would have conducted *me*!'

0 1 Starting with this extract, how does Dickens present ideas about responsibility in the novel?

Write about:

- how Dickens presents the attitude of Marley's Ghost towards his own responsibilities
- how Dickens presents the importance of responsibility in the novel as a whole. **[30 marks]**

Stage One: Decoding the question

2   Begin by **highlighting the key elements** in the question that you need to address.

You could complete the table started below.

Key element in question	AO covered	What you need to do
attitude of Marley's Ghost…responsibilities	AO1 – your understanding and response	Focus on finding evidence about Marley's Ghost and…
How does **Dickens present**	AO2 – what the writer does	Focus on *what Dickens does* – his language and structural choices

Stage Two: Gathering the evidence (AO1)

3   Now gather evidence:

- Jot down **three or four key quotations** from the **extract** that help with your response.
- Then jot down **three or four key references** from **the text as a whole**, which also help answer the question.

Stage Three: The writer's effects (AO2)

4   Choose some of your quotations or whole text references and decide what you are going to say about:

- Dickens's choice of vocabulary or other language
- Dickens's use of structure.

Stage Four: Considering context (AO3)

5   Now consider **ideas about context**.

- Do any of your listed points or quotations link clearly to social, cultural or political ideas related to Dickens or the Victorian period in general?
- Think about ideas related to the theme of social responsibility and how you could comment on Dickens's views in this regard.

Stage Five: Write a quick plan

6   Now decide what points you are going to make now under these headings:

Extract	Novel as a whole
1.	1.
2.	2.
3.	3.

Stage Six: Write your response

7   Now write your response to the exam-style question. Remember to follow your plan.

Peer- and self-assessment

Assessment objectives
- AO1, AO2, AO3

....

1 Read the following sample response to the exam-style question on page 128 and the examiner's comments and overview.

Student C

At the start of the extract, Marley's Ghost 'cried' out as he explains the pain of regretting what he'd done in his life. This shows that he realises now that he could have done more to help people. This is how Scrooge will feel too as the book goes on.

AO1 – attempt to provide overview of theme, linking to Scrooge

The way Dickens has presented Marley is that he knows he is being punished because he failed to do the right thing. This is why he is 'double-ironed', which means he is wearing heavy prison locks on his feet, probably to remind him of his crime. This crime was to miss 'one life's opportunity misused', which means he had all his life to do good but chose not to. Again, Dickens makes it clear that Marley regrets this when he says, 'Yet such was I!' This is a warning to Scrooge not to go down the same path but take responsibility for his fellow humans.

AO2 – effective explanation of a relevant quotation

AO2 – explains writer's choice

However, the most important part of the passage is when the Ghost says, 'Mankind was my business', in response to Scrooge. This has a double meaning because Scrooge was referring to Marley as a 'good man of business', meaning a successful one. But the Ghost criticises Scrooge and says 'business' means concern for others. Dickens seems to be stressing the message that wealthy readers should take responsibility for the poor, not abandon them.

AO2 – beginning to explore interpretation of Dickens's use of specific phrase

AO3 – straightforward reference to Dickens's message

In the rest of the novel, Scrooge slowly gets a sense of responsibility. At first he thinks trade and money are the most important things. When he sees himself talking with Belle, he probably thinks he should have been responsible for her, as she was poor. But he thought only of himself.

AO1 – clear signal of switch of focus to the rest of the text

Later, when the Ghost of Christmas Present shows Scrooge the two children Ignorance and Want, Dickens is saying that society is responsible for them. Not very many children went to school and lots were working in factories even from the age of seven or eight years old, so Dickens is showing what happens if society turns its back on poor people and children.

AO1 and AO3 – attempt at more detailed exploration of contextual background

There is also the part with Fezziwig. Scrooge talks about Fezziwig having 'power' – which is a bit like responsibility to make people happy. He begins to get the message that he can change the world for the better, which is what he does in the final Stave, taking responsibility not just standing by and doing nothing.

AO1 –important new point but requires further development

Examiner's comment

This is a solid response that shows understanding of the idea of responsibility in both the extract and the novel as a whole. There are some suitable references to quotations, mostly expressed fluently, but the response lacks close analysis. There are two relevant contextual links, but in the same way that the language is rarely explored in depth, so is the case with these links.

2 Evaluate this answer and decide which of the two levels (Grade 5 or 7+) from the AO marking criteria table on pages 122–123 it is closer to.

3 Now read the next student's response to the exam-style question on page 128.

Student D

If there is one word that sums up Dickens's message in the novel it is 'responsibility'. Written as a response to the appalling conditions Dickens himself had witnessed that the poor lived in, and designed to rattle the comfortable lives of fellow Victorians, the text continuously promotes the idea that 'Mankind' is everyone's 'business'.

AO1 – opening topic sentence sets up a conceptual view of the task

AO3 – fluent link in to contextual background to the novel

Those words of Marley's Ghost, in this passage, remind the reader and Scrooge that 'business' is a word with multiple meanings. In an age of rapid industrialisation, a time when fortunes could be gained through the trade of cotton, metals, coal and so on, 'business' would be seen by many as an unquestionable virtue. Here, Marley's Ghost rubbishes that suggestion. 'The common welfare was my business', he states, regretfully. Marley feels this all the more painfully because he was a man of trade, a man who had the money to help. The metaphor that his everyday work was a 'drop of water in the comprehensive ocean of my business' stresses how unimportant making money was against the wider responsibility to 'charity, mercy, forbearance, and benevolence'.

AO1, AO2 and AO3 – convincing bringing-together of contextual message, with detailed analysis of language

AO1 and AO2 – detailed understanding of language use and effect

Marley also draws attention to the vast workings of God and the universe in the use of adjectives such as 'immortal' and 'incessant' and contrasts them with the 'little sphere' within which humans operate. This punctures Scrooge's self-importance and inward attitude, yet also touches on how 'kindly' gestures – even in that tiny world – can have undreamed – of consequences.

AO1 and AO2 – close analysis leading to interpretation

At this point in the novel, of course, the penny hasn't dropped as far as Scrooge is concerned. Despite having seen the Ghost weighed down by cash-boxes and padlocks, he is yet to make the connection between the actions he takes and the impact on others. That is to come. Slowly, over the course of the Staves, Scrooge begins to see that 'responsibility', or the lack of it, has fateful outcomes.

AO1 and AO2 – fluent linking highlights structural effects

As Dickens's own father abandoned him to work in the blacking factory, so too Scrooge's father abandons him to a hated school. Seeing himself as a boy there, Scrooge 'wept to see his poor forgotten self'. He understands at that point parental neglect, a point made all the more poignant by the care and love lavished by Bob and family on Tiny Tim.

AO3 – further relevant reference to Dickens's life

Dickens also presents other positive images of responsibility. Fezziwig has the 'power', with the expense of relatively little money, to make people happy or sad. He provides a party not just for his employees but also for local workers misused by their own employers. Scrooge begins to understand that he has this power, too, if he chooses to use it responsibly.

AO1 – succinctly expressed link to other moments in the text

By the end of the novel, the Ghosts have all shown Scrooge how hollow his words from Stave One were. 'It's not my business', he tells the charity collectors. But the impact of Scrooge's turning away from society and responsibility are shown to bring shame, loneliness and death. This was Dickens's message to his readers – that, even if invisible to them, many suffered. If they took a moment to look behind the cloak, they would be shocked to see the frightening visions of Ignorance and Want.

AO1 and AO2 – perfectly chosen final quotation to link passage to novel as a whole

AO1 – original interpretation rounds off response perfectly

Examiner's comment

This is a compelling, convincingly argued response that demonstrates a real overview of the text, but also detailed understanding. The references are exceptionally well chosen, and links are made throughout between extract and text as a whole. The references to context add significantly to the argument and enable the student to analyse and interpret throughout. All in all, this is a sustained, highly effective response.

 4 Evaluate this answer and decide which of the two levels (Grade 5 or 7+) from the AO marking criteria table on pages 122–123 it is closer to.

In what ways is Student D's answer a more effective response than Student C's?

Apply what you have learned

Look again at your own work and follow this process:
- ✔ Read the two sample answers by Student C and Student D and the examiner's comments.
- ✔ Look again at the AO marking criteria for the Grade 5 and Grade 7+ responses (pages 122–123).
- ✔ Evaluate your own response and the level you think it is closer to.
- ✔ Then, find a paragraph in your work that you think requires improvement or development.
- ✔ Identify which aspects from the AOs you need to improve in your chosen paragraph.
- ✔ Re-draft or rewrite the paragraph, applying the changes you think are needed.

Revision and practice

Checklist for success

Before the exam:
- ✔ If time allows, re-read the novel thoroughly alongside this companion.
- ✔ Using the companion, select and learn two or three key quotations for each character and each theme.
- ✔ Talk about the text and your ideas: speaking out loud can help clarify your thinking. For example, speak to a friend for a minute on topics such as 'What do I know about the theme of poverty in the novel?'
- ✔ Practise writing quick plans on sample questions.

In the exam:
- ✔ Read the extract quickly but thoroughly.
- ✔ Read the question, highlight the key words and then skim-read the extract again, highlighting any key quotations you could use that are relevant to the task.
- ✔ Write a very quick plan (or compose one in your head), detailing what points you will cover from the extract and the rest of the novel.

Remember:
- ✔ Include at least three points on the extract itself.
- ✔ Comment on the wider novel (so, ideally focus about half the essay on the extract and half on the novel).
- ✔ Keep your focus on what Dickens does – his use of language and structure – and explain the effects of his choices in relation to the task.
- ✔ Consider how Dickens's methods or the actions/events you identify link to wider contextual ideas and themes.
- ✔ Write in clear paragraphs, explaining your thoughts, and giving evidence to support them.
- ✔ Use quotations. Make sure you put them inside quotation marks, embed them in sentences and keep them relatively short (no long sentences or paragraphs).
- ✔ If you can, try to offer your own interpretations or insights.

Acknowledgements

The publishers gratefully acknowledge the permissions granted to reproduce copyright material in this book. Every effort has been made to contact the holders of copyright material, but if any have been inadvertently overlooked, the Publisher will be pleased to make the necessary arrangements at the first opportunity.

An extract from *Bad Blood* by Lorna Sage, Harper Perennial, 2000, pp.21-22, copyright © Lorna Sage, 2000. Reprinted by permission of HarperCollins Publishers Ltd; The figure 'English Life Expectancy 1840-1935' Data source: Office of National Statistics. Published in *The UK Public Works Loans Board: central government loans for local government investment*, Finance Brief 6 by R. Franceys, September 2015, Figure 2. Public Finance for WASH, www.publicfinanceforwash.org; An extract from "Some Christmas Thoughts", *The Spectator*, 27/12/1845, p.13, http://archive.spectator.co.uk/article/27th-december-1845/13/some-christmas-thoughts. Reproduced by permission; An extract from "Want to volunteer to help homeless people this Christmas?" by Derek Mace, *The Guardian* 13/12/2013, copyright © Guardian News & Media Ltd 2017; An extract from *Black Jack* by Leon Garfield, Oxford University Press, pp.16-17, copyright © Leon Garfield, 1968. Reproduced with the kind permission of Johnson & Alcock Ltd; An extract from "Education in England: a brief history" by Derek Gillard, http://www.educationengland.org.uk/history/chapter02.html, © copyright Derek Gillard 2011.

The publishers would like to thank the following for permission to reproduce pictures in these pages:

Cover images: Classic Image/Alamy

p11 Pictorial Press Ltd/Alamy Stock Photo, p13 Granger Historical Picture Archive/Alamy Stock Photo, p14 Pictorial Press Ltd/ Alamy Stock Photo, p15 Pictorial Press Ltd/Alamy Stock Photo, p16 Granger Historical Picture Archive/Alamy Stock Photo, p19 World History Archive/Alamy Stock Photo, p20 Lebrecht Music and Arts Photo Library/Alamy Stock Photo, p21 Classic Image/ Alamy Stock Photo, p23 Chronicle/Alamy Stock Photo, p25 Pictorial Press Ltd/Alamy Stock Photo, p27l Jack Sullivan/Alamy Stock Photo, p27r Chronicle/Alamy Stock Photo, p29 Classic Image/Alamy Stock Photo, p31 Granger Historical Picture Archive/Alamy Stock Photo, p37 Niday Picture Library/Alamy Stock Photo, p38-39 Granger Historical Picture Archive/Alamy Stock Photo, p41 Pictorial Press Ltd/Alamy Stock Photo, p42 Trinity Mirror / Mirrorpix/Alamy Stock Photo, p45 Niday Picture Library/Alamy Stock Photo, p46t Classic Image/Alamy Stock Photo, p46b Niday Picture Library/Alamy Stock Photo, p47 World History Archive/Alamy Stock Photo, p48 Pictorial Press Ltd/Alamy Stock Photo, p51 Niday Picture Library/ Alamy Stock Photo, p53 The Granger Collection/Alamy Stock Photo, p57 Everett Collection Historical/Alamy Stock Photo, p59 World History Archive/Alamy Stock Photo, p60 Chronicle/Alamy Stock Photo, p63 Classic Image/Alamy Stock Photo, p64 Pictorial Press Ltd/Alamy Stock Photo, p66-69 Everett Collection Historical/ Alamy Stock Photo, p70 Niday Picture Library/Alamy Stock Photo, p71 Andrew_Howe/Getty Images, p74 World History Archive/ Alamy Stock Photo, p75 Philip V Allingham/The Victorian Web, p77 Andrew_Howe/Getty Images, p81 Moviestore collection Ltd/Alamy Stock Photo, p83 mexrix/Shutterstock, p84 Lebrecht Music and Arts Photo Library/Alamy Stock Photo, p87 Chronicle/Alamy Stock Photo, p90 Gubin Yury/Shutterstock, p93 Lebrecht Music and Arts Photo Library/Alamy Stock Photo, p94 Niday Picture Library/Alamy Stock Photo, p104 World History Archive/Alamy Stock Photo, p106 Andrew_Howe/Getty Images, p107 Photo 12/Alamy Stock Photo, p108 Rebekah J/Shutterstock, p110 Niday Picture Library/Alamy Stock Photo, p112 Classic Image/Alamy Stock Photo, p114 Photo 12/Alamy Stock Photo, p115 19th era/Alamy Stock Photo, p116 UniversalImagesGroup/Getty Images, p117 Gábor Páll/Alamy Stock Photo.

Notes

Notes

Notes

Notes